MERRITT WATTS is a graduate of the Medill School of Journalism at Northwestern University. Her first job was telemarketing; she is now a writer in San Francisco.

HANYA YANAGIHARA lives in New York City.

First Jobs

First Jobs

True Tales of Bad Bosses,
Quirky Coworkers, Big Breaks,
and Small Paychecks

Edited by Merritt Watts

Series Editor Hanya Yanagihara

Picador
New York

www.picadorusa.com
www.twitter.com/picadorusa • www.facebook.com/picadorusa
picadorbookroom.tumblr.com

Picador® is a U.S. registered trademark and is used by St. Martin's Press under license from Pan Books Limited.

For book club information, please visit www.facebook.com/picadorbook club or e-mail marketing@picadorusa.com.

Designed by Omar Chapa

The Library of Congress Cataloging-in-Publication Data is available upon request.

ISBN 978-1-250-06125-6 (trade paperback)
ISBN 978-1-250-06130-0 (e-book)

Picador books may be purchased for educational, business, or promotional use. For information on bulk purchases, please contact the Macmillan Corporate and Premium Sales Department at 1-800-221-7945, extension 5442, or write to specialmarkets@macmillan.com.

First Edition: May 2015

10 9 8 7 6 5 4 3 2 1

Editor's Note

These stories come from oral interviews conducted with each subject. The stories have been edited and adapted for length and clarity. The names and identifying characteristics of some persons described in this book have been changed, as have some places and other details of events.

Contents

When Opportunity Knocks: The Success Stories

When It Couldn't Get Worse: The Horror Stories

When Life Hands You Lessons: The Things We Learned the Hard Way

When Business Meets Pleasure: The Fond Memories

Introduction

"Hello, I'm calling to see if you have just ten minutes to take a brief survey today."

In the summer of 2004 I repeated that sentence dozens of times every hour. I was working as a telemarketer trying to get investment bankers to take a survey about their health benefits. It was my first job.

Every afternoon, I would put on a headset, press a button, and the machine would start autodialing one number after another. I would hold my breath and hope no one would answer, saving us both the pained exchange that was to follow in which I would optimistically ask them if they'd like to take my survey and they would inevitably reject me.

Sometimes people would hang up immediately upon hearing my opening line, sometimes they'd have an excuse, like "Uh, now's not a good time, can you call me later?" This

ded them to the "interested" list, which
ally have to call them again even though we
that wasn't getting us anywhere. My favorites
people who simply said "no"—they went directly
not interested" list and would never hear from me
One banker actually screamed at me "Ten minutes?!?
you know how much money I could make in ten min-
tes?!?" I thought that was a fair point.

Over the course of the entire summer, I got just six people
to take the survey. The last one was a guy who seemed nice
and was responding well to my ultra-professional telephone
demeanor. He was doing a great job with the survey, even
taking long pauses before answering, which I assumed indi-
cated he was giving his responses some real thought. And
then I heard the toilet flush.

Talking to someone while they, ahem, do their business
isn't exactly the stuff career dreams are made of, but it's nothing compared to some of the tales in this book. In the year I
spent interviewing people about their first jobs, I heard some
truly horrifying stories. There's "The Zoo Chef" (page 124),
whose experience cooking for animals involved a walk-in
freezer full of dead rodents; the victim of "The Holdup"
(page 12), who was held at knifepoint over the counter of
a quaint card shop; and "The Very Personal Assistant" (page
34), whose responsibilities included picking up a drunk boss
at a strip mall.

There were plenty of encouraging stories too: "The Pecan-
trepreneur" (page 67), who started a nut business that net-
ted him enough money to make a down payment on a home;

"The Rosie the Riveter" (page 200), whose time in the ship-yards during World War II made her feel proud and independent; and "The Striving Shoeshiner" (page 77), who went from shining shoes on the street to becoming the mayor of Los Angeles.

Nearly everyone I interviewed for this book said they had embarked on that first job with money on their mind—they wanted a paycheck and a little pocket change, maybe enough for a car. But almost nobody could remember what they actually *spent* that money on. "I guess going to the movies . . ." and "probably just junk" were two common responses. On the other hand, nearly everyone I talked to could recall their biggest accomplishments—or most embarrassing mistakes—on the job. It wasn't the money they earned or the stuff they bought that stuck with them; it was the experiences. And as they reflected on their early days from their current vantage points (which included a corner office, a director's chair, a conference room at their namesake company, and even a comfortable recliner during retirement), they found they were remarkably still applying the lessons they learned during those decidedly unglamorous first jobs.

I was also surprised to find that there might be a real, scientific reason why our first job experiences make such an impact: About a decade ago researchers discovered that a teenage brain goes through a period of growth that is second only to the development we experience in the first eighteen months of life, when we learn to walk and talk. That's a pretty big deal, biologically speaking. This second period of growth gives us the opportunity to form thousands of new connections between neurons, increasing our ability to learn. But this time around, instead of learning how to put one foot in front of the other, we're learning how to interact with people, make decisions, socialize in different environments, plan for the future, manage our emotions, and set and achieve goals . . . all that fun frontal-lobe stuff.

Now here's the catch: Our brains may be primed to grow up, but in order to actually develop these sought-after skills when we are young, we have to get out of our comfort zones and enter the real world. Reporting to a boss, handling difficult customers, planning a schedule, showing up on time—these are the tasks that create and exercise new neural connections during that key learning period, and can actually rewire our brains to resemble those of responsible adults.

The lesson here is to not underestimate the influence of a first job. Take, for example, scooping ice cream. It's the quintessential all-American summer job, and you may think the only thing you'd learn at an ice cream shop is how to properly top a cone with rainbow sprinkles. But I interviewed three former scoopers for this book and their stories couldn't have had more different conclusions. In "The Ice Cream Shop Education" (page 153), a Midwestern teen was (spoiler alert!) ultimately fired from her scooping gig, but not before learning a few things about negotiation and management that MBA students pay good money for. In "The Slacking Scooper" (page 132), a high school cheerleader learns what it feels like to absolutely hate a job, which compels her to find something she is passionate about and that eventually leads to a fulfilling career. The "Serious Scooper" (page 63), on the other hand, conquered her paralyzing shyness to become the best ice cream scooper in the shop and now has her own incredibly successful chain of ice cream stores and an award-winning line of ice cream. Three teens doing the same job, three very different takeaways.

After a year of talking to people about their first jobs, I sat down to sort through all my interviews and edit the stories. I quickly found that my book about first jobs was not actually about first jobs at all. It isn't about the scooping, sweeping, weeding, or delivering; it is about awkward beginnings, painful endings, embarrassing moments, epic failures, public humiliations, secret achievements, amazing bosses, and early rebellions. In short, it's about the kinds of hard-earned lessons that are worth way more than all of those early paychecks combined.

—Merritt Watts

WHEN WORK GETS WEIRD

The Strange Tales

The Nude Model

2002

Everyone is surprised when I tell them that I was a nude art model in college. I don't really project that sex kitten persona that most people associate, wrongfully I might add, with nude models. My standard outfit for a Friday night out in college was jeans, a polo shirt, and flip-flops. I had never done any modeling before—I'm pretty short, so it's not really my bag—and I'm not even an artist.

But when I started college at Penn State, I was on the hunt for a really good part-time job. My parents are both solidly middle class and I knew I'd need to pay my own way through a lot of college. The on-campus jobs all paid minimum wage, and the off-campus jobs took more time. I was really into spending my waking hours doing schoolwork and getting As, so that wasn't going to work. I was looking for a job where I'd make the most money in the least amount of time.

One of my new dorm friends was an art student and she was the one who tipped me off to the nude modeling gig. She described it very simply: You sit there naked and people paint or sculpt your form. Once she mentioned that the models were paid fifteen dollars per hour, I was sold. I went over to the art building and filled out the application. It was pretty easy— basically if you are willing to do it you are hired.

My first job was for a sculpting class. I was so nervous that my palms got really sweaty just walking into the building. I kept thinking, "What are they going to think of me? Are they going to think I'm a slut? What kind of girl takes her clothes off for money?" I was really worried about people having that perception of me. The only thing that calmed me down was reminding myself that all of these people were aspiring artists and I was doing something very valuable for them.

Still, that first time was pretty awkward. I went into the bathroom to disrobe but, once I took off all my clothes, I realized that the classroom was across the hall and I'd have to run naked through the hallways to get in. So that wouldn't work. But it also felt weird to just strip down in front of people. Eventually I got a robe that I would wear so that I could change in private and walk over to where I was posing before taking it off.

I'd be asked to pose differently, depending on the class. Sometimes I'd sit on a pedestal, and sometimes the pedestal would spin around and I'd feel like I was on a lazy Susan. Other times it was really active; I'd be asked to hold a position for thirty seconds and then switch. That was meant to be a practice for students who were learning to draw differ-ent lines and curves quickly. My favorite position was the odalisque position. It's a very classic pose where the woman is reclining. That was the most comfortable because all I had to do was lie there in a nest of pillows. Sometimes the instruc-tor would put on music and I would just fall asleep.

The students were always in a circle around you with their mounds of clay or their notebooks or easels. You can't really see what the students are drawing or sculpting; the only thing you can see is a room full of people looking at you. I'd often peek at how people drew me and a couple times I thought, "That's not how I look!" But generally people want to draw something beautiful so they focus on your positives, and you end up looking like a better version of yourself.

I was told I was pretty good at it because I was able to keep still. You don't think about how hard it is to stay still but it's actually quite physically demanding. I would leave sore and numb. But I started really looking forward to the time I spent modeling. It evolved into a Zen-like activity. At that time cell phones were just becoming a thing and they made me feel constantly busy and distracted, so it was a nice refuge to just be able to zone out.

I was pretty popular with the professors and so they kept hiring me and I ended up doing it a couple times a week for three years of college. I was only recognized once, at a frat party. I didn't recognize him, but obviously he recognized me. We were both very mature about it, I think, and so there wasn't much else to be said. Otherwise, I didn't really have a lot of friends who were art students, so I was able to keep my modeling pretty separate from my social life.

I'm not an artist, but I learned that drawing the human form is one of the most difficult things to do. It takes a ton of talent and a ton of practice. And behind every great master-piece or work of art there is someone who got paid to pose for that artist.

—ALYSIA MUELLER, *thirty, has worked as a reporter at the Associated Press and as a communications special-ist for USAID in Amman, Jordan. She is currently employed as a staff writer for a law firm in New York City, where she lives with her husband and her baby daughter.*

The Mexican Minor Leagues

2003

I played a lot of baseball growing up in El Centro, a small town in California about ten minutes from the Mexican border. It would get crazy hot there in the summer, but my dad would still take me out to throw baseballs every day. As a result, I had a pretty good high school baseball career, at least up until my senior year. That was the year that all these kids from Mexicali came over for high school and joined the baseball team. They were good. *Really* good. Five of us lost our starting positions right away. We had held that team together for the past three years, but these other guys were just *so* much better than us. And they were great students too. They did everything right. I wanted to hate them, but I couldn't.

That year, we won the last game of the season, which

made us league champions. We did it—we won it—but the five of us didn't play at all. I sat on the bench the whole time. I didn't even feel excited when we won because it wasn't really my team anymore.

As I was leaving the game that day, the dad of this kid I grew up with came up to me and said, "Hey, Jeff, I'm starting a team in Mexico. Do you want to play this summer?" He said we would have games in Mexicali once a week on Sundays, and that I would get paid twenty-five dollars a game, free meals, and a ride. I was in.

Sunday at 6:00 a.m. they rolled up in a really nice SUV. I had no idea what was going to happen, I didn't even know what to bring. I just showed up in a T-shirt, baseball pants, and my jock strap. They handed me a team jersey that said "Diablos" and we headed down to Mexico.

We played around Mexicali all summer. We played teams from Tijuana, San Felipe, and other towns around there. Mexicali is surprisingly gigantic, and we'd travel everywhere. One week we'd be playing in the middle of a field and no one would watch us, and the next week we'd be playing in a good-sized stadium with lots of people who paid to see us. My hometown was close enough to Mexico that these were just day trips; sometimes my dad would even come watch us play.

As promised, we always got food. No matter what, we always got fed before we went home. But if you had a really bad game, you didn't get paid. It wasn't even talked about. It was just, like, you struck out three times, you are *not* getting twenty-five dollars. And other times, if you had a really good game, you got a six-pack of beer. That is kind of awkward when you're eighteen. I mean, it's not a trophy or anything, it's just a warm six-pack. It's kind of a hard thing to take home to your parents.

Everyone on the team was under thirty, but I was one of the youngest guys. I was also the only white guy on the team and I had surprisingly little Spanish comprehension. I didn't understand most of what was going on. But I knew the cuss words, so I knew when someone was mad at me. Our coaches spoke broken English so they could tell me what to do, but if they were giving a rousing speech before the game, I would pretty much just stand there and wait for them to say "Break!"

Being white, I also got hit a lot. Pitchers would throw the ball right at me because they thought it was funny. Looking back, yeah, it was kind of funny. Hit the white guy—that's a game, let's get the crowd into it! I get it. But at the time it upset me so much. I would always steal second base, or at least try to, because I was so mad at the pitcher. It was my little revenge.

One game there was an *actual* baseball player on the other team. This guy was legit. Back in the day he had pitched for the Pittsburgh Pirates, but now he was over forty and still trying to make it. He was obviously the best player on the field. I had never been in competition with a guy who could pitch so hard. He would just fling balls across the plate. As I was getting ready to go up to bat and face this guy, our player on first base hurt his hamstring and had to come out of the game. At that point, we were out of players.

It was ridiculous; people were *paying* to watch us, and we had run out of baseball players. So my dad stood up in the stands and said, "I can play." My dad was fifty-five at the time, six feet tall, and probably a hundred fifty pounds soaking wet. He was wearing this big lifeguard hat, jeans, and a collared shirt. But he ran out there, someone threw him a jersey, and he stood on first base. Everyone was like, "Is this real? Can you do this?" But the person who was the most upset was the pitcher. He was like, "I am a *professional*, and you are going to let this person just come onto my field? No!" He was mad and he was having it out with the umpires. I was the only white guy on the team, so it was obvious that it was my dad. And I was up to bat next.

The pitcher threw three fastballs at my head. *Super* fast. I was scared to death. My dad was encouraging me from first base, saying, "Stay in there! Stay in there!" He even stole a base, so then he was on second. Then the pitcher sent one right down the middle. I swung, hit a double, and my dad scored a run! So then I was on second base and the pitcher was even more pissed off. I have never been so scared. I was still convinced he was going to try to throw a ball at me. The next guy on my team comes up to bat and the pitcher hits him with a fastball right in the side. I have never seen a player crumple like that. He basically had to crawl to first base, but he had to stay in the game because we were so desperate.

In the end, the other team won. But hitting a double off

a legit pitcher and scoring in my dad—that was one of my all-time favorite moments on the baseball field.

>—JEFF, *twenty-nine, tried to walk onto his college baseball team during his freshman year. Now he is an elementary school teacher for children with special needs and an avid baseball fan.*

The Holdup

1990

I grew up in Baltimore, which can be a little . . . bumpy. In an effort to give me a straight shot in life, my parents were pretty protective. When I turned sixteen I wanted to get a job so I could have my own cash, but my parents were really picky about where I could work. All the other kids were getting jobs at ice cream shops, restaurants—fun places where kids could hang out, places that were a little social. My parents were like, "You will have no part of that."

Eventually I found this ad in the paper for help at a card store in the little strip mall about five minutes from my house. It was just two little old ladies running the store, selling cards and figurines and other little tchotchkes. My parents finally said okay, and I got the job.

At the shop I usually did a bit of inventory and helped get things organized, but the biggest part of the job was helping clueless men pick out presents for their spouse or their mother or whomever. It was a lot of walking guys around the store asking them questions like "Well, what does she like? What are her hobbies?" I liked that the store was all about celebration—people came in for birthdays and anniversaries, that sort of thing.

One day I was working with one of the owners. She was doing inventory in back while I worked at the cash register up front. This guy walked in and he started looking in the glass case underneath the register where we had the fancy pens and things like that. He asked to see one of the pens. I remember clicking into salesgirl mode, like, "Well, let me show you, mister!" When I was distracted getting the pen out of the case, he moved behind the counter and put a knife to my side and told me to open the cash register.

In that moment, everything started moving really, really slow and I thought, "Okay, I'm not going to make that fatal mistake of forgetting how to open the cash register or anything." I just got really focused and did exactly what he said: I unlocked the cash register and gave him all the money. Then he ran out.

I don't know if I was in shock or what, but as soon as he left I walked to the back of the store and calmly told the owner, "We've just been robbed." I wasn't crying or hysterical. I just said it very matter-of-factly. In fact, I think I said it so matter-of-factly that she was suspicious. She was like, "What are you talking about?" So I said, "Come look in the drawer, all the money is gone."

As soon as she looked in the drawer I think she was

wondering if I had pulled a fast one, if I had pocketed all the money and just made up this story. She really didn't believe me for a beat! But then we called the police, and they came and said that it was not the first incident like this one in the past couple of days in that area. So that kind of validated me. But if I had been a little more hysterical I think it would have been better for me, at least in that moment.

When I told my parents about the holdup, they couldn't believe it. They were shocked. They had done all this thinking and planning and hand-wringing about my job and here I was with these little old ladies in a store that sold teddy bears and "I Love You" balloons and this happened. Needless to say, that was the last day I worked at that card store. My parents made a new rule: No more jobs at strip malls. So I got a job at a different card store in an enclosed mall. Two years later I moved to New York City to live on my own. Out of the frying pan and into the fire!

—SHERRI BROOKS VINTON, *forty-seven, is a cookbook author based in Los Angeles. She has written three books about canning and preserving produce.*

The Pet Gravedigger

1998

When I was two years old my dad got out of rehab and we moved down to Florida. He was just looking for a job that had steady pay—you don't have a great amount of leverage when you're fresh out of rehab. So he started working at The Humane Society in Boca Raton, Florida. At first, he was the guy who drove around in a van to pick up dangerous animals in people's yards. He had a big, long stick with a rope around the end that he'd use to pull alligators out of people's pools and that sort of stuff.

Eventually he was at that for long enough that they put him in charge of the pet cemetery. I had never heard of a pet cemetery before, but it was exactly what it sounded like: a place where people could go to bury their pets and come back to visit the graves. By the time he got that job I was thirteen and I wanted to start working. He wasn't in the greatest health anymore, and I could help him out. Plus, he paid me. So I started going to the pet graveyard most weekends and some days after school.

Digging the graves was my main job. A grave for a medium-sized dog would take three to four hours to dig. My dad had devised a system for this: He had different pieces of plywood shaped to the different-sized caskets. I would lay that plywood on the ground to start the grave off, like a stencil. And then I would take it off and dig deep. Not a six-foot-deep grave or anything—I don't think you'd want to dig anything six feet deep in the Florida muck—but, like, three or four feet deep. It was a lot of work, especially for a kid.

Once I dug the grave, I'd have to get the animal ready for burial. There was a big freezer behind my dad's office where we'd put the dead animals so that their bodies didn't decay too much.

My first burial was a golden retriever. Now, that is a very heavy dog, especially when it's frozen. I had to take it out of the freezer a bit early to let it thaw, because it had frozen in such a position that it wouldn't fit in the casket. I was wearing gloves, but it was a typical hot day in Florida, so I was also wearing short sleeves and sandals. I lifted the dog up and tried to carry it so that it didn't touch any of my bare skin. The hair on it was all stiff and matted. I was pretty grossed out. Then, all of a sudden, I felt a drip on my foot. I still remember the way that felt, and it makes me shudder. It was so cold and creepy-feeling—some unidentified liquid dripping off of a dead, defrosting dog. I wore closed-toed shoes from then on.

If someone wanted an open casket funeral—which, trust me, people did—you'd have to let the animal thaw out a bit first. You'd usually have to set it out for a few days; those animals could really freeze all the way through. Then you'd try to set the animal up in a sort of natural-looking way. There was this little room in the office with a coffee table that we would turn into a makeshift altar. I'd put a little white table-cloth on it and my dad would put the pet in the casket on top of that.

Just like in a real funeral home, people would come to view the body and say good-bye. Everyone got very emotional about their pets. Sometimes my dad would say a few words based on what they had told him about the pet beforehand. He would close the coffin and then play some new age-y flute music. It sounds very funny, but people would really appreciate what my dad did.

It doesn't sound great, but my main emotion during the pet funerals was probably bafflement or confusion. People seemed to be *looking* for something to be sad about. I mean, you care about your pet, of course, but I always thought there must be something a bit unhinged about a person who would have a full-on pet funeral, not to mention pay good money year after year to keep their pet grave maintained.

Eventually, I stopped working at the cemetery. When I was thirteen, I was really happy just to be able to go there and spend time with my dad, but by the time I was sixteen, I was just embarrassed. I had made the transition from child to teenager and working at a pet cemetery had become a source of shame for me.

A lot of people start getting into arguments with their parents when they are teenagers, but I never really had that problem with my dad, and I think it was because I had a lot of respect for what he dealt with day to day. We moved to Florida because he had a drug addiction and I feel like everything in his life after that has been about making it up to us. When I spent time with him at the cemetery, I learned how hard he worked. Yeah, he complained after a long day, but he never asked for anything different. It shaped my perception of him forever. I never really built up a lot of resentment for him, which a lot of other kids whose dads left when they were babies might have.

Strangely, I also think it gave me a sense of a job being something that should help people. That was the thing that stuck with me about watching my dad at work. People could turn to him when they were grieving their pets. I would make fun of them a little but my dad really helped them and they were always so grateful for the experience he created. The fact that he was able to take that seemingly menial role and make it into something that was meaningful really influenced me, and I think it's part of the reason I ended up in a helping profession too. When I think about my career now, it's important to me that I feel good about whatever job I'm doing, even more so than making a lot of money. My parents always stressed the idea of doing something that you care about, and that really stuck.

> —JESSE KOVALCIK, *thirty, is a licensed marriage and family therapist and a school counselor. He does not own a pet.*

The Barkeep's Revenge

1975

When I left college I ended up in San Diego, where my parents lived, but it was not the right place for me. There was a street called Vacation Village Boulevard and I think that says it all about San Diego: I just couldn't take the place seriously. So I resolved to move to the East Coast. I got some rides and hitchhiked all the way to Washington, DC, and showed up on the doorstep of my friend who was in medical school at George Washington University.

I was crashing on his floor next to a furnace, and I knew the first thing I needed was some money in my pocket. That was how I ended up with a job as a barback at an old DC bar. This place was an institution that had been around for years. It was dark inside and everything was made of wood. The bar was about eighty feet long and behind it was a collection of three-hundred-year-old beer steins. It was around the corner from the Treasury so that was a big part of the clientele; it was decidedly a gents' hangout.

Being a barback involved just the worst kind of work. You had to load up all the ice for the bartenders, drag kegs out of the basement whenever the bartenders told you to, bus all the tables, that kind of thing. This was a really old-school place so they had bartenders who had been there for years and they chewed up the underlings pretty badly, right out of the chute. It was kind of a trial by fire: They saw how much crap they could give you and how much you were willing to take. It was like a hazing and the only way to survive was with a lot of "yes sir" and "no sir." At the time all the barbacks were young guys out of college, just like myself, who knew what we were getting ourselves into. The goal was to work your way up to the hallowed status of bartender, and so you had to pay your dues.

This place had a lot of little alcoves and nooks and crannies and it was my job to clean them all. One day, as I was sweeping in the back, I saw Dustin Hoffman over in a dark corner. I recognized him immediately. He was already pretty famous at this point; he'd done *The Graduate* and *Midnight Cowboy*. He was chatting intently with another guy and I was just minding my own business. Then, out of the blue, he looked over at me, made eye contact, and said, "What are you, the token Jew?" Which I was. And so I said, "Yeah, as a matter of fact, I am." He kinda liked the answer and we got to chatting.

It turned out that out he was working on his directorial stage debut; it was a play called *All Over Town* that was showing right around the corner. He asked me if I wanted to check it out and I said, "Sure, if I'm not working." So I wrote my name down for him and he said he'd leave two tickets at the box office for me.

When I went home and told the buddy I was staying with this story, he couldn't believe it. He thought I had totally lost my mind. I said, "Come with me to the play and then you'll see." So we go down to the theater the night of the show and we walk up to will-call. I'm half expecting this to be a practical joke, but there they are: two tickets in my name. My friend is just in shock.

We were seated six rows from the front, right in the center. We watched the first half of it and I just thought it was hilarious. At the intermission, as we were walking out to get some overpriced drink in the lobby, Dustin Hoffman came right up to me and said, "Hey, you came, that's great! I can't believe it. How do you like the play?" By this time, my buddy, a very serious type in med school, was totally flipping out. Keep in mind that I had been in town for about three weeks at this point and here I was hobnobbing with Dustin Hoffman. We both told him we were loving the play, it was great, it was fabulous, all that. He said, "Well, I hope you continue to do so, and why don't you come to the after-party? Be my guest." And I said, "Sure, where is it?" and he said, "Oh, it's at the place I met you at, the one around the corner . . ." The bar where I worked.

I was a little awkward about that because I had been working there for only a few weeks and there was a whole pecking order going on and all that. But I thought, "To hell with it, this is a once in a lifetime opportunity. I'm going to go ahead and show up and be a partygoer by invitation. What are they gonna say, 'No, you can't come in because you work here?' I'm with Dustin Hoffman!"

Sure enough, my buddy and I showed up after the play with Dustin Hoffman and we got some looks from the rest of the staff that, uh, to be polite, were rather withering. But we were hanging out with all the big shots from the play, trying to make intelligent conversation with the playwright, that kind of thing. It was a really great night.

The next day I went into work and one of the managers, who was a particularly snotty guy, got all bothersome with me about it. He said, "You have to get permission if you're going to come in here as a customer." I just feigned ignorance. I said, "Oh, gee, I thought it would be okay. I mean, a pretty famous guy invited me, so . . ." But I could tell my days there were numbered and I bailed on the job another pay period after that.

I was too much of a wiseass at the time to understand the idea of bartending as a career; I thought I should get everything I wanted right away, you know? My own self-worth was a bit inflated, and the Dustin thing didn't help. I felt like I should be able to short-circuit that whole process even though I had not paid my dues.

Now I work at the front of a house at a restaurant where we get a lot of politicians and celebrities and whatnot. I have it in my mind, somewhere in my life, that Dustin Hoffman and I are going to cross paths again, and while I'm not ego-tistical enough to think he'll remember me personally, he clearly will remember the first time he directed a stage play,

so I'll prompt him with that. Forty years later, it makes for a
pretty amusing story.

> —EVAN REYNOLDS, *sixty-three, spent twenty years as*
> *a hotel concierge in Washington, DC, where he has met*
> *the Dalai Lama, Hillary Clinton, and Crosby, Stills &*
> *Nash.*

The Corrupt Carny

1997

I was a teenage hoodlum. My hair was dyed bright pink and I liked to spike it up really high so it would poke out the top of my visor. I wore thrift store T-shirts all the time; my favorite was one that had Mr. T's face on it that said "Mr. T-Shirt." Yep, I was that guy. Plus I had braces and terrible acne. So when I started to work at a carnival the summer before high school, let's just say I didn't exactly look out of place.

I grew up in the suburbs south of Chicago, where carnivals are a big deal. My best friend's dad got us both jobs on the local circuit, which was a great idea on his part because otherwise we would have just run around terrorizing people all summer. Our favorite activity was filling water guns with grape soda and then riding around on our BMX bikes hosing people down. That's a ton of fun, by the way, because the carbonation in the soda creates a permanent spray so you never have to pump the water gun.

Anyway, Illinois is one of the biggest weekend carnival states and there are tons of companies that operate independently and supply rides and games to all these festivals. These companies would come to town for the carnival and recruit a little army of kids to help work it—we were carnies in training.

My first day they told us to come in at eight in the morning, but the festival didn't start until noon, so I was wondering what we'd be doing. Turns out, there was plenty to do because our task was cleaning up the grounds from the night before. Oh, the smells, the stuff you'd find in the grass . . . It was disgusting. But that was just paying your dues. See, there are four stages of being a carny. There's cleanup, which is what all the kids and the beginners do. Then there's the inflatable games. The people who work at inflatables literally just babysit children most of the time. The next step up is the classic carnival games. Then there are the rides, but that's really only for the top-tier carnies.

I was just a fledgling carny, but I made friends with a few of the real ones. They are the kind of people your parents tell you to stay away from. Real carnies are the modern-day gypsies. They just travel around the Midwest and take a cut of whatever cash is made at the carnival. No permanent address, no savings account. Next time you're at a carnival, look around and you'll notice that there are no middle-aged carnies: Either you've been a carny for life or you haven't been broken in yet. Then there are the really old guys who have the war stories about carnival accidents. Everyone in my circuit talked about this one carnival in a grocery store parking lot where the Zipper ride tipped over. That was the stuff of legend.

After I did cleanup crew for a bit, the carnies started giving me other stuff to do. I moved up to the inflatable games, and my specialty became the inflatable boxing ring. This was my favorite one because people would be boxing, having a great time, and not even notice that their wallet had fallen out of their pocket. I wouldn't necessarily pickpocket, but . . . I'd pick the wallets up off the ground. It was a trick I learned from the older carnies, of course.

I'll always remember the last time I ever took a wallet. The wallet was canvas with a Velcro closure, the kind you have when you're a little kid, and I tore it open. There was like seven bucks in it, and I took the cash out and brought the wallet to the Lost & Found. Then I went straight to get my forty-dollar pay for the day. It was the first time I ever felt guilty for stealing. I used to shoplift gum on the way to school and all that, but this was the first time I actually felt bad. I thought, "These people are paying me to do something and I'm being shady." That was an important life experience for me, to feel the shame of my actions early on, because I changed from that.

I spent a few weeks in inflatables, but then I moved on to the real games. Those games were the pinnacle of my youth carny career. Not everyone moves up to games because one of the things you're supposed to do is to make the game look easy to get people to play. I could do that because I was born with carny skills!

I had the carny job for about two years, on and off, and my favorite thing about it was getting really good at the carnival games. In my youth, I thought I would be a charmer, that women would come by and I would impress them with my skills, and I'd help them win the giant stuffed panda bear. They would totally fall for me. Strangely, it didn't work out that way.

—CHRIS WOODY, *twenty-nine, is a director at a major marketing firm. His milk jug skills are still superb, though underutilized.*

The Accidental Showbiz Beginner

1968

My life has been totally serendipitous. You know how some people say, "I want to be a journalist" or "I want to be an actor"? For me, it was nothing like that. In college I studied engineering and ended up in history, but the only thing I knew when I graduated was that I wanted to leave the country, so I traveled for a while. When I came back my father was all over me to finally get a job.

I had just one cousin who was successful in the corporate world and my father said to him, "You gotta get this kid a job." The cousin had a friend who worked at NBC and he got me a gig as a correspondent at *The Tonight Show Starring Johnny Carson*. It was the lowest-level job in the entire place, except for maybe the receptionist, who often had to babysit the animal acts.

There were two correspondents and it was the kind of job where, if you didn't get promoted out of it within a year, you were going nowhere. You were supposed to leave. It was a big deal to get it, but it was still bottom of the barrel.

As a correspondent, you weren't really a part of producing the show. Your main responsibility was answering the fan mail, the stacks of ridiculous handwritten letters like, "My husband and I love watching your show, it's our favorite, can you send us $1,000 for a new car?" I really couldn't have cared less about these letters. In fact, I once typed out about three hundred response notes with the word "sincerely" spelled wrong; I spelled it "sincereley." The office manager said, "You can't send this out," and I said, "Why not? It's only one word!"

And then there was the "crazy phone." It rang all the time—anybody could call and talk or complain. You were not allowed to be the one who hung up first. You had to listen and you had to log these inane complaints about how some guest had offended them. Another big complaint was that the volume automatically went up when the commercials came on. Then there were the personal conversations about their leaky faucets, their pets, how their dog was feeling, and, of course, how they were feeling. (And let me tell you, they were never feeling good.) These conversations would go on forever because the kinds of people who called the crazy phone had nothing better to do.

Johnny Carson had his offices somewhere else in the building. He always wore these crepe-soled shoes, so you wouldn't hear him when he came in, but then all of a sudden the room would go dead silent. The boss. He was not a bad guy, but he was the most taciturn, stiff person you ever met in your life, the complete opposite of his Mr. Charisma TV persona. One time I had to sit outside his office to answer his phones. It was like a tomb in there. He might have said hello, but I'm not sure.

Fans used to complain that Johnny Carson was never on the show, that he took a lot of time off. But I loved this because then I would get to be the *de facto* assistant to the guest hosts sometimes. This pretty much involved ordering food from the Stage Deli for them and overhearing their conversations. But it was wonderful when I had someone like Woody Allen, Peter Lawford, Bill Cosby, or Flip Wilson. Once I had Milton Berle. He was on the phone getting one-line jokes from some writer and I had to write them down as he got them. I was disillusioned. I always thought he wrote his own jokes.

Woody Allen asked me to listen to his whole monologue because he was so nervous, which was really kind of great. Of course, I can't stand anything about him now, but at the time I thought he was fabulous. One of his wives was named Louise, which is how we bonded. If he had said, "Run away with me to Zanzibar," I would have been waiting at the backstage door. A lot of the guest hosts had this self-important, patronizing attitude, but he was so respectful and funny, definitely my favorite.

The assistants sat in a bullpen in the middle of the office. They were all young, beautiful girls who walked around barely dressed. Finally someone put out an edict that you couldn't wear a see-through blouse without a bra, that's how far things went.

The other correspondent who had been there two years was a sweet girl, but she was going nowhere. She'd go off with a particular repeat guest host whenever he filled in for Johnny. Then she'd show up the next morning wearing an expensive necklace, or a new bracelet, or something like that. There was another girl, an assistant, who was having an affair with a married movie star who was pretty big at the time and she would carry on and on about how he was going to leave his wife, but he just couldn't right then. Yeah, right. She'd get a lot of flowers. (Clearly the girl getting the jewelry was smarter.)

And then there was Marcy, the assistant to the producer John Carsey. Everyone joked that if Marcy married John she'd become Marcy Carsey. Well, guess what? She did, and she ended up producing some major TV shows like *The Cosby Show, Roseanne,* and *Third Rock from the Sun.*

I did have a brief affair with a writer for the show. It was kind of fun shutting that office door. The writers used to get six-week contracts and they were being paid eight hundred bucks a week, which was a fortune back then. At least I thought it was a fortune; I was making ninety bucks a week. They would have a meeting every morning and they had to have ten jokes ready to present to Carson. He would sit there and listen and either laugh or not laugh. Writers are always wrecks, but they were all extra nervous before this meeting.

I only lasted six months as a correspondent—I wanted

to go traveling again and when I was passed over for a promotion I had my perfect reason.

When I was there I really didn't appreciate how special it was. *The Tonight Show* was a big deal, a legend, and it could have been a stepping-stone to a career. If I had stayed at NBC, who knows? But that just didn't register at the time.

My parents were resigned when I quit. They were wonderful, loving, and tolerant, but they were never particularly impressed with anything I did. I'm sad my father never saw what I eventually accomplished, but my mother was around for it. When I wrote my first book she said, "It's so short, who is going to pay money for this?" At my book party someone came up and said, "You must be very proud," and she said, "You should meet my son!" So no, *The Tonight Show* as a first job did not impress them; they were just glad I finally had a job.

—LOUISA ERMELINO, *sixty-eight, is an author and the vice president and reviews director at* Publishers Weekly. *A collection of her stories will be published by Sarabande Books in April 2016.*

The Very Personal Assistant

2003

I grew up in a town that was famous for having one of the largest office parks in the country, so when it came time for me to get a job I was pretty sure it would be in an office somewhere. I went into our school resource center and looked through a white binder full of different job offerings in the area. All the pages were torn up and stained from a million kids looking through them, but there was one page that was brand new. It was for a part-time assistant job at a real estate company.

The office was right off the service road of a highway, in a little shopping center with three other buildings. It had four desks and two conference rooms. The walls were entirely pink and there were seashells everywhere. The interview process

was really easy: They clearly wanted a girl because everyone else who worked there was a woman, so, by virtue of having two X chromosomes and a car to get me to the office, I
got the job immediately.

I started working after school for a few hours, but this
silly little part-time job became a job I had for the next six
years, and the place where I worked every summer during
college. It became like a really demented family. A really, really demented family.

The owner was this woman Patty, a big, voluptuous
woman who was a real ballbuster in the office and, I got the
sense, in her personal life too. You couldn't have a conversation with her without hearing about how much she hated her
ex-husband. She was a curvy woman with big, blond hair—
the kind of color that you get out of a box—and long fake
nails. She had a boob job and I *know* she had a boob job because about a month in she lifted up her shirt and showed
me, to see how I felt about the scars. They were pretty hei-
nous, but of course I lied and said they looked great—I mean,
she was still the boss. She would wear tiny little outfits and
try so hard to look feminine, but it never quite worked, probably because she'd do things like sit in her office and tweeze
her chin hair. She was kind of like a man in women's clothing, which is the nicest way I can put it.

Patty liked to wear big, heavy earrings and one day they
split her earlobe open. So my job that afternoon was to research surgery and find out how annoying it would be for
her to get her ear fixed up. In the meantime, she had a business lunch so she just put her hair over her ripped-up ear,

put a big clip-on earring in the other ear, and went to the lunch. I have to give her credit for never letting her insane problems hold her back.

Patty had a boyfriend, which I found out about because she said, "I had sex on the conference room table last night, so when you have your lunch, just eat it in the other conference room." So I went in the other conference room and I added "clean the table" to my to-do list. At the time I didn't really think it was weird because I thought it was *so* cool that she had her own business, and you know what, if I ever have my own business I'm going to have sex wherever I want!

We were at this really fortuitous time when real estate was booming and she was doing great for herself. She had a really nice house and a little red convertible. Some days I'd get to drive out to her house in her convertible to pick up a different outfit for her if she didn't like what she was wearing.

One of Patty's main ambitions was to get back at her ex-husband and get full custody of her daughter. Her ex was never around—he was kind of a delinquent dad—but he would never admit it in court. So we rigged up a tape recorder to go in her underwear and she met him at a gas station. They had a whole fight for like an hour where she tried to get him to confess what a bad parent he was. Afterward, she came back and gave me the tape recorder that had been in her lady parts. We worked together to transcribe it, but all you could really hear was the rustling of her underwear. In the moment it felt like *Law & Order*, you know? We were hunched over the tape player like, "What did he just say? If we can't get that word we have nothing!" Meanwhile, we couldn't even legally record him without his permission, so the whole plan was really going nowhere in court.

One day I had to pick her up at a sex toy store because she had gotten too drunk at a business lunch beforehand. I had never been to a sex toy shop, I hadn't even had sex at that point! So I'm looking around all wide-eyed thinking, "Ooooh, this is for bad girls, this is a bad-girl store." I think she got a kick out of that.

It all seemed kind of wild and fun to me, and only years later did I realize how sad it all was. Looking back on it now, I can see that the convertible she drove wasn't actually that expensive, and her house was big, but I can't imagine she owned it. I mean, if you're a real businesswoman you're not getting drunk at a strip mall lunch and then getting picked up by your high school–aged assistant. But at the time I just thought it was great that she did what she wanted to do.

I did learn silly skills that served me well in the end, like proper e-mail correspondence and how to use the phone. And for all the demented things that happened, Patty really taught me how to not be stunned by anything. There's nothing you can say to me that will be as shocking as a forty-five-year-old woman asking my opinion on whether or not her nipples were put on correctly.

—A., *twenty-eight, is a manager at a large digital news corporation in New York City.*

The Starstruck Salesgirl

2004

My plan to get a job in Aspen, Colorado, where I was spending the summer before college, was to stroll the streets and find a really hip clothing boutique or a cute shop or a cool local bakery that needed help. There's plenty of that kind of thing in Aspen, and my best friend had secured a similar job a few weeks beforehand. It was going to be great.

I soon discovered that there were no more openings because it was already too late in the season. Finding a job would be a lot harder than I thought. I quickly got kind of desperate because I only had ten weeks of summer left and I needed to make some money, not to mention have something to do. So I started taking it street by street, very methodically, inquiring at every single place.

"Inquiring" was basically just me dressing up, walking in, and asking if they had any work. I had a résumé but there's not much you can say when you've never had a job before, so I think I focused more on the fact that I was going to college, had full-time availability, and was a really quick learner.

I don't even know why I chose to enter Curious George, because it's immediately clear what kind of store it is. There are taxidermy animal heads everywhere. There's an entire wall of guns and a half wall of knives. In between there are a lot of little trinkets and some Native American turquoise. But I walked in there and did my little spiel and the manager said, "Actually, we are hiring," and asked about my schedule. They liked the fact that I had nothing else to do and that I could start immediately, so that was it: I had the job. I felt excited to start working, though I didn't know if I would like working *there*, necessarily.

The shop was named after the owner, George, who was a local and was in Aspen before it became this very fancy, touristy place. George did not really fit in with the current feel of Aspen; he was a true Colorado cowboy who liked guns and knives. He had a *huge* handlebar mustache and always seemed to have a little can of wax with him that he would use to smooth and shape it while staring at himself in the glass display case. He would smooth his mustache over and over again; it was a process that seemed to last forever. You would know he was almost done when he moved on to his eyebrows. Now those kinds of mustaches are considered cool and hipster, but I am here to tell you that George was doing it before it was cool.

The first few weeks of work were pretty slow. I got to

know George and the manager, but I was pretty shy. I think I was really intimidated by the surroundings: all those guns and those huge animal heads! Sometimes I would just look at the taxidermy and think, "That is so sad, that poor animal. What was it like? How did it die?" Obviously I could never admit that to anyone else at work.

One day George called the store and said, "Has Bill Clinton come in yet?" and I was like, "Um, no." He said, "Oh, well, we're expecting him, so make sure everything looks good." I hung up and thought, "Yeah, *right*, there is no way Bill Clinton is about to walk into this place." George was a pretty weird guy, so it was no surprise that he was talking crazy talk, right?

I brushed it off and the manager and I ordered Chinese takeout for lunch. It was a really slow day, so we spread our food out all over the counter and were just chatting and eating, a normal lunch break. And then, all of a sudden, in walks Bill Clinton. He had bodyguards all over him and the whole cobblestone street in front of the shop was filled with black Escalades. We shoved our Chinese food under the counter so quickly.

President Clinton walked around for a bit and I basically just tried to look busy while secretly studying him. I guess he had come in to buy these little marble sculptures called fetishes. I don't know much about the art form or history of these fetishes, but apparently he buys one there every year. It's really too easy. I mean, Bill Clinton and a fetish? Come on.

I wasn't waiting on him, my manager was, but as he was

leaving he shook my hand and looked at me really sincerely and said, "Thank you, have a great day." His handshake was distinctly unpresidential. It was really floppy and warm. I told my mom this later and she convinced me that it was a handshake he had adopted specifically for these kinds of situations, because if he was to give a good solid handshake to everyone he met, he would probably hurt his hand. That seemed reasonable.

Once Bill Clinton left, my manager and I could not stop talking about it. It was the most exciting thing that had happened to me all summer. We were still reviewing every detail and laughing about it twenty minutes later when Arnold Schwarzenegger walked in.

Arnold did not have any black Escalades outside, no cars or anything. He had just been biking around town and decided to stop in. At this point he was the governor of California, but you would have had no idea he was a big deal, except for the huge crowds that started to gather outside. There were about a hundred people peeking in our windows!

Arnold was with his son, who was probably ten or eleven at the time. They were looking around and they wandered over to the gun wall, where I had decided to stand and pretend to polish the guns. They walked over my way and I got so nervous, the whole thing suddenly felt really surreal.

Arnold asked to see a certain rifle. Now, I don't know anything about guns. I don't know the lingo, I don't know how to talk about guns, and I don't know any of the different types or brands. Somehow I managed to find the gun he was pointing at and I handed it to him. Arnold was talking to his son, telling him about the different parts of the gun and how you load and unload it. Then, without meaning to, his son pointed the gun right at me. Arnold freaked out. He swooped and yelled, "No, no, no, you *never* point a gun at a person!" I was just standing there. They immediately left, without buying anything.

To this day, those are still my two biggest celebrity sightings ever. That slow afternoon at a very weird job turned out to be the best story of that summer.

——BLAIR SCHWAB, *twenty-nine, is in graduate school for speech pathology. She returned to Aspen a few years ago and found that Curious George had moved into a smaller location. Most of the taxidermy has been replaced with art.*

The Dating-Service Receptionist

1991

The summer after my first year of college I registered with a temp service. When I found out that I had been assigned to work in the office of a video dating service I just started cracking up. I thought it was crazy that people would try to find dates by watching videotapes! But a temp service will send you anywhere that needs a bit of help. I'd already had a few short gigs that involved shredding paper in a back room all day or putting random files in alphabetical order. I figured that at least the video dating service would be less boring!

Video dating was the nineties version of online dating. To join, you'd pay a fee and then come in to film your video. The video was just you talking about what you were looking for in a partner, telling them a little bit about yourself and what you liked or didn't like. Then you could go into a huge room filled with other people's VHS tapes that had their names and vital stats written on the label. Someone would lead you to the area for people in your age range and you would pick a few that sounded interesting. You could watch them in a screening room right there in the office or check them out and take them home, just like you were at Blockbuster. On Friday nights the dating service hosted mixers where everyone would come and have cocktails and check each other out in real life.

My job was to sit at the front desk to greet people when they came in and to check their membership cards. It was definitely a lesson in being professional. People were coming in with their heart on their sleeve just hoping to find love or at least a date, which was really sweet. I had to be as polite as possible in sort of an awkward situation. I mastered the art of joking around with people without crossing the line, just making it a welcoming and relaxing place.

There were definitely a couple of guys who confused my friendliness. They'd say, "So, are you a member?" and I'd reply, "Oh, I'm not old enough to be a member." That shut it down pretty quickly. It worked out nicely to have a quick way out without having to be rude to a client.

I befriended the guy who made the videos; he was a film major who was just a couple of years older than me. He wanted to be a commercial film director, and this was his idea of great practice. Whenever someone would come in to film their video I would run over to him as soon as they left and ask, "What was her tape like?" or "What did he say?"

I never got to actually watch the tapes, but he did put together a "blooper reel" of all the best outtakes, and one night we watched all the material from the cutting room floor. It was hilarious, but also a huge learning experience from a dating perspective. The guys always went wrong when they were trying to describe what they wanted physically. They'd be like, "You know, not too fat." Stuff you're not really supposed to say because it comes off so badly. With the women it was a lot of insecurity stuff. They would spend tons of time talking about their flaws and what they're not good at. And, to me, it was really obvious: Don't talk about what you *don't* like about yourself, keep it positive and focus on the good things. Simple stuff.

I always thought that the real life mixers were the most fun. Everyone was in a good mood because they were about to get their drink on and chat people up. I always made a special effort to tell the ladies how nice they looked. I'd say that I liked their shirt or dress or whatever, because they had clearly put some effort into that and I wanted to make them feel as good as possible before walking into the room.

One time a guy named Joe checked in and asked, "Have you seen Mary? Is she here?" and then a few minutes later Mary came and asked, "Is Joe here? Which one is he?" I thought to myself, "That one might work out!" When they left together I knew it had gone well. That was the only match I ever witnessed.

Working there was fun but I definitely had a sense of "Oh man, I hope I never have to do that." I just couldn't figure out why these perfectly nice men and women couldn't meet dates in a more normal way. A few years after I left the dating service, VHS as a technology just disappeared. Then the Internet took over and, not long after that, online dating started.

—MELISSA O'NEIL, *forty-two, is a senior manager at an online media company. She met her boyfriend of four years online.*

The Odd Jobs

1965

When I was a teenager in Brooklyn I decided I needed a job, mainly so that I could have some money to go to the Village and dance my feet off at the clubs. A counselor at my high school told me about Manpower Inc. It was a place for getting casual jobs, mostly manual labor, and though I didn't have any experience I figured I could handle it.

On my first day I checked in at the headquarters in Manhattan at 6:30 a.m. The procedure was to check in at the front desk and then hang around until they had a job for you. So I'm waiting there, wondering if I'll ever get any work, when they announce, "Oh, we've got something for you." Terrific!

The job was to wash a wall at Horn & Hardart, one of the automated restaurants New York City had at the time. They're not around anymore, but these places were beautiful. They were kind of like cafeterias where office workers could go and have a good, quick lunch, but to get your meal you would walk up to a wall of stainless-steel cubbyholes filled with the highest-quality food you could imagine, all freshly cooked. You picked what you wanted, put in a dollar or two, opened the glass door, and got your New York steak or your baked potato.

My instructions were to check in with the kitchen when I got there, so I walked into this huge, busy facility filled with cooks and dishwashers, all Haitian men, and announced that I was there to clean the wall. They all turned and looked at me with this confused, inquisitive expression. Then they started asking questions like "What did you come here for?" and "Where are you from?" I explained that I was a high school student on summer vacation and this was the job they sent me to do. Immediately they said, "Oh no, you're not going to wash the wall. You're in school? You're not going to wash the wall. Come over here, sit down. Do you want some coffee?" I think they felt that, because I was a student and was getting an education, I should not be washing walls, that I was above that. It was such a fuss!

So I spent the whole day just hanging out in the kitchen talking to people instead of working. I got a tour of the whole restaurant, got to see how all the food was cooked and put on a conveyor belt that went into the cubbies. They said, "What do you want for lunch? You can have anything you'd like." So I asked for a steak. The guys were just incredible and the whole day was nuts. At the end of it, I got paid and they washed the wall. A job well done.

The next day I reported back to Manpower and was sent

off to a different job, this time at a warehouse in Midtown. It was a very large warehouse packed with electronic equipment and I was supposed to open all the boxes filled with last year's inventory and smash it against a wall. It was everything you could imagine: stereos, turntables, portable radios. There were boxes full of this stuff, just stacked ten or fifteen high. Why? Because the new stuff had come in. Simple as that. New equipment came in and they weren't allowed to sell the outdated stuff anymore. There was no recycling or anything at this point, so I'm sure they just took it all to the dump. It was truly as wasteful as it sounds. After a day or two, destroying these electronics started to get routine, even boring. Open the box, pick up an item, smash it against the wall. Open, lift, smash. Open, lift, smash. Over and over again.

My last job with Manpower was disassembling the New York World's Fair. I had been to the World's Fair with my family as tourists, and I never thought about how it would all get taken down, but, as it turns out, that was done by men like me. My entire job was to move just piles and piles of rebar from one side to another, all day. I never saw it completely dismantled—I went back to school before it was finished.

—ROBERT SOTO PLA, *sixty-eight, got a bachelor's degree from San Francisco State University and a master's from Harvard. He is a retired teacher and a social worker in California.*

WHEN OPPORTUNITY KNOCKS

The Success Stories

The Junior Journalist

1944

I grew up in Pekin, a town in central Illinois that got its name because the founders thought they were on the opposite side of the world from Peking, China. I was interested in journalism since the age of twelve. I don't know how, but I just knew it was what I wanted to do. I got involved in my school newspaper during junior high and it just stuck. I loved it.

When I was a sophomore in high school, the sports editor for our local newspaper, the *Pekin Daily Times*, was drafted into World War II, so he asked me if I would be interested in his job. He knew I had been the editor of my school paper already and so he was pretty sure I'd be interested. I didn't know enough to say, "Are you kidding? I'm sixteen!" so I just said, "Sure!"

Jack brought this idea to the publisher. There really weren't many men around at that point, most were going to

war. The publisher had hired women to fill all the other positions at the paper but I guess he did not want a woman as
the sports editor; he'd rather hire a child.

The publisher and the editor of the paper interviewed me.
I don't remember much about the interview, but I must have
made an acceptable impression because they offered me the
job. I think it was about June of 1944 when I found myself
sports editor of the *Pekin Daily Times*—a paper with a cir-
culation of about fifteen thousand.

There were only two other men in the office: the publisher, who was too old to get drafted, and a guy who did
farm reporting, who had a medical condition. Then there were
more than a dozen women selling ads and writing stories.
None of them really looked twice at a teenager helping to put
out the paper.

I had to put out an entire sports page every day of the
week, except Sunday, all by myself. To get it done before
school I would wake up at about five o'clock. We were ra-
tioning our gas during the war so nobody was driving cars.
I would walk about half a mile to the newspaper office. I'd
be the first one in so I'd use my key to open the office and
turn on all the lights. It felt like quite a responsibility.

It was a big, open office, a classic newsroom, with the
printing presses in the basement down below. If I was there
around two or three o'clock in the afternoon I would feel the
whole building suddenly start to shake as the printing machines kicked on—that meant we were going to press. It was
a thrilling feeling, and I still remember it vividly.

Some days, I had covered sports events the night before

and I would have stayed up late writing about them, or would be writing about them that morning. The two big teams that we covered in Pekin were the high school sports and, in the summer, church league softball. The office had a United Press Teletype that would send the national news early in the morning. I would look at all the sports news from the Teletype and decide what we should put on the sports page. They always had a great baseball roundup and everyone liked to read about University of Illinois football.

Then, when the ad department came in, they would tell me how many ads we had sold and that determined how much space I had available to use on the sports page. I would fill it up with stories I had written and wire copy, and I'd write all the headlines. Then I would take my copy back to the one Linotype operator who happened to be very knowledgeable about sports, thank God. He caught a couple of real blunders that I had made. After the Linotype operator reviewed my page the compositor would put it all together and give me a proof to review. We had a proofreader but the proofreader didn't come in until later, when I was at school. So I was pretty much in charge of writing, editing, and proofing the sports page. By about ten o'clock I'd be finished and ready to go to class.

There was no one really teaching me how to be a professional editor. I worked on my two school papers so I knew how to write a lede and how to write a headline. I just transferred what I had learned on those two papers and it worked.

Friday-night football was a big deal in Pekin, so of course I covered it. I had to get the story in the paper the next day so I'd always go write it up as soon as the game was over. I'd walk to the newspaper office, open it up, turn on all the lights, and sit there and write the story while all my classmates were out having fun and celebrating. They'd come by our office every now and then and bang on the big glass window and make faces at me as I worked my ass off. But those were the stories everyone wanted to read the next day; they were always my longest and most carefully read stories of the week.

I remember once the publisher himself had gone to the game. He saw my story before it went to press and called me over and said, "Dick, you didn't say anything about the defensive player Les Haney, and what a terrible game he played!" Well, I didn't think it was all that terrible, plus I had to go to high school with Les Haney and all of his teammates. The publisher rewrote a few things in my piece and I thought, "Well, this is the end of me." But the football players weren't that upset. In fact, they acknowledged that he was probably correct in his analysis.

I often had to cover the wrestling matches of my twin brother, Jim, who was on the team. There was one particular tournament I remember when Jim was wrestling a student from a different school and, suddenly, his opponent did what's called a switch: It's when you make a quick move and throw your body over the opponent in order to get the advantage. When he did this, in this very quiet gymnasium, you heard a loud *POP!* That was the sound of my twin brother's shoulder blade breaking. Honest to God, you could hear it crack.

Jim fell back onto the mat and his opponent, with a look

of horror on his face, pulled away. The coach ran out to Jim, who was flopping around on the mat. Now, what did I do? What does a sports editor do when his twin is out there in agony during the wrestling match? I sat at the press table and I took notes.

I figured that was what I was there to do. Plus, it might embarrass Jim if I ran out there. So I just stayed back and did my job. There was a delay in the wrestling competition as they took him into the dressing room and waited for the ambulance, so I took that opportunity to find out how he was. He was pale as a ghost at that point, but he was okay. That night I wrote about the match and I didn't make any big deal out of the injury, I just noted that one of the wrestlers was taken to the hospital and was out of the tournament.

For the rest of my life I have agonized about the moment Jim was hurt and I did nothing. But every time I brought it up with him, Jim just dismissed my concern. There wasn't much I could do, he said, his wrestling career was over anyway. But it was my decision that day that made it clear that I was cut out to be a real journalist.

In the newspaper office of the *Pekin Daily Times* there was a sign on the Teletype that said something like, "The War Department Rules prohibit looking at the United Press Teletype material because classified material is sometimes transmitted." The federal government would often tell newspapers when there was a big war event about to happen later that day so they could plan to put it on the front page. The Teletype often had this type of material that was okay for journalists to see, but not anyone else. That gave me the proudest

feeling in the world. It's part of that sense of being a journalist that you are someone special and you learn things
other people can't. I'd get a tingle up my spine every time I
looked up at that sign; it was like, "Here I am! I know more
than anyone else in this town!" It was a great feeling.

I worked at the paper for two years, from summer 1944
to summer 1946. I was a member of the newspaper staff at
the end of the war, when the atomic bomb went off and the
Japanese surrendered. The United Press Teletype clicked away
all day and during much of the night. The experience made
it clear to me that this was what I wanted to do. I never even
considered anything else.

—RICHARD STOLLEY, *eighty-six, studied journalism at
Northwestern University and worked for* Life *maga-
zine in Atlanta, Los Angeles, Washington, DC, and
Paris before becoming the founding editor of* People
*magazine. He was named to the American Society of
Magazine Editors Hall of Fame in 1996.*

The Printing Professional

2002

I was born and raised in Tehran, Iran. After high school I went to get my associate's degree in communications at a school in Shahrud, about a six-hour drive away from home. My father was helping me with money the first semester, but I come from a very poor family, and it was tough on my parents when I was a student. So I was out there looking for a job without having any experience or skills. I didn't know how to do anything.

One day I noticed that students at my school, including myself, were always searching for printing shops where they could print out their projects. The school was very old and it didn't have any of the modern facilities that we consider standard now, like a computer lab with printers. So I decided to start my own printing business.

The first step, of course, was to buy a printer. I did a lot of research on the best kind. The print shops that everyone was going to had those huge laser printers, and the quality on those was just awful. Everyone complained about it; I knew I had to do better. I ended up finding an inkjet printer, which was considered very high quality at the time.

The price of the printer was the exact cost of one month's rent. I went to talk to my landlord and told her that I was having difficulties that month, that the rent money never came from my father and that I would need a little more time. It was a lie, but she agreed. I took the money my dad sent me that month and bought the printer instead of paying my rent.

I brought my new printer on to campus, set it up, and started printing everything for students. To set my prices, I looked at what other print shops were charging, and I did it for 10 percent less. After a few weeks, everyone knew about me. People heard how I was printing things at a really high quality and for a really cheap price. Of course, when the school found out, they got upset because I was selling to students on school property, so they kicked me off campus and I started doing it out of my apartment.

There were hundreds of students, and my business was just me and one printer. I was so busy. My hands were always stained from the cartridges and there was ink all over my body, but I made so much money that I was able to pay my own rent and then even help my sister when she needed money.

My parents were very excited about my venture. They called me all the time and asked, "Are you sure you don't want money? Are you sure you are making enough?" It felt really good to say, "Yes, I'm totally fine, don't worry about me."

This was all fun until finals—then it got really tough. I had so many customers that I honestly couldn't sleep. The printer was analog, so there was no way for it to tell me "the yellow cartridge is low right now." It didn't communicate like that. I had to check everything as it was printing. Instead of sleeping I had to watch each page as it was coming out of the printer. If I didn't catch a low cartridge in time, a whole job could be ruined, which would be a waste of ink and paper. And then on top of all that, I had to do my own finals. It was crazy.

Shahrud, where I was living, didn't really have a dependable place to buy ink cartridges when I needed a refill. So I developed a system: Whenever my friends went back to Tehran to visit their parents I would give them two free prints if they would refill my ink cartridge when they were in the city. That was the only way I could make sure I always had enough ink.

When summer came, all my business dried up because the school was closed. But I had so much money saved that I bought a car and drove it as a taxi, which became my next job. When I bought the car my friends joked with me and said, "This car is made from our money! It is built of our school projects!" We all laughed, but I knew it was true, and so did they.

—SHAHROUZ VARSHABI, *twenty-nine, moved to New York and received an undergraduate degree in graphic design and a master's in design technology at Parsons– New School in New York City. He still stores his old inkjet printer at his parents' house in Tehran.*

The Serious Scooper

I feel like I was born an adult. I've been a very serious, very high-output person for as long as I can remember. When I was a kid in Peoria, Illinois, I would pick cattails out of a ditch, dye them, and then weave baskets to sell. When my grandmother taught me how to knit I made a bunch of Barbie sweaters and sold them to every kid in the neighborhood. When I was in junior high I found out that if you blended sugar and Kool-Aid mix together in a food processor you could fill straws with it and make pixie sticks. I called these Axl Rods, named after Axl Rose, and I sold them at school for twenty-five cents a pair.

Making and selling things was just part of what I did growing up. I didn't want to make one thing, I wanted to make a hundred, and I wanted to turn it into something that other people would want. I think it was partly that I enjoyed making stuff, and partly that I enjoyed being productive.

So I had already had kind of a long career before I got my first job at the ice cream shop, which I started the day after I turned sixteen and was legally allowed to work. The thing is, even though I operated like an entrepreneur from a young age, I did it despite the fact that I was shy. Really, deeply, painfully shy. At school I would throw up before giving speeches. I took an acting class to help me get over my shyness but all I did was fake laryngitis to get out of it.

Everyone told me that Meryl Streep was also really shy, so when I got behind the ice cream counter I channeled Meryl Streep. I just tried to re-create her personality so I could become a great ice cream scooper, the same way she was a great actress. I didn't want to bother anybody or be some big ice cream nerd. I wanted to be the person that I would want to have helping me if I was ordering ice cream: someone who was really professional and really knowledgeable. So I learned everything about the ice creams. I learned the perfect way to scoop. I knew everything about the company. Mastering that was very important to me because it made me less shy and it helped me to do my job without anxiety.

I loved working. I wanted to work as much as I possibly could and I didn't even have anything to spend the money on. I spent it all on my friends—I really did. I'd take everyone out to eat with my money; I just didn't care about it at all.

The less pleasant part of the job was that, when I was working there, girls were not treated fairly. The owners, these two men, would say out loud, "No, you're a girl, you can't mop the floor. No, you're a girl, you can't count the money." I fought through it, though. I didn't ask for anything; I just kept showing up on time and doing all my jobs well. First they let me mop the floor. And when I mop a floor I *really* mop a floor, you know? I do a good job. Then one day I finally got to count the money; I was really proud of that.

Eventually, the owners actually gave me the key and put me in charge of opening the store one day. That was a big deal. That was a *huge* deal. I had the key! But the day I got that key I went to a baby shower with my mom and somewhere the key fell out. I scoured the house and the car, I went back to the baby shower, I retraced my steps, but I couldn't find it. I lost the key, just completely and totally lost it.

I was disgusted with myself, and so embarrassed. I had to call the owners and say, "I'm sorry, I know you gave it to me yesterday, but I already lost the key." It was a painful phone call. I thought they should have said, "You're fired, that's ridiculous, you had *one* job to do," but their response was really nice. I was in tears when I hung up the phone because they were so kind to me about it. I'm sure they could tell by my voice that I felt awful because I took that job really seriously.

There are people in the world who wouldn't have freaked out about losing the key because they think that something like scooping ice cream is a small, unimportant job. I can tell you, those people aren't good at what they do. I think that attitude turns them into victims. You think, "Oh you poor person, you have to go somewhere menial that you hate every day, for five hours or seven hours and that is so tragic for you." I never wanted to be that way; I wanted to be the opposite. No matter how small the task, I wanted to be the best at it because I knew that put me in a position of power. And even back then I thought, "You know, I can complain about it, like all the other kids here at work, or I can be the best at it." By the time I left I really felt like I was an expert and even if it was just mopping floors I had standards and that defined me and made me confident.

—JENI BRITTON BAUER, *forty-one, is a James Beard Award–winning cookbook author and owner of Jeni's Splendid Ice Creams, an ice cream shop that she founded in Columbus, Ohio, and now has fourteen locations across the country.*

The Pecan-trepreneur

1962

I got into the nut business when I was twelve years old. It started as just a small door-to-door operation, but then it took on a life of its own. Originally, selling pecans was my father's idea. He always thought I should be industrious, so he hatched the plan with me. When school got out that summer I sat down at my mom's electric typewriter at home in New York and wrote to every pecan company in Georgia I could find to ask for samples and pricing.

As soon as the samples came in, I inspected them all very thoroughly. I wanted to be sure that the nuts came in full halves, not pieces, and I wanted nice-looking packaging. I knew that how well these nuts were presented would make a big difference. I got my order in for delivery on November 1, just in time for all the holiday baking to begin.

That first year I rode my bike around the neighborhood, going house to house and giving my sales pitch. I would hold the one-pound cellophane bag of pecans in my hand and I'd just say, "I'm selling pecans. Would you be interested in buying some?" I think my delivery got a bit better as I went along, but I always kept my pitch very simple.

I was successful that year for two reasons: First of all, I was a cute twelve-year-old. That's hard to turn down. Second of all, I had a product that people couldn't get in the grocery store. At that time, you could get those tiny bags of pecan pieces in the baking aisle, but that was it—no pecan halves, which were what really impressed people.

That first year I had sold out of pecans by December 15. It was just six weeks of work and I was flush with cash. I had so much cash that my dad required that I tithe 15 percent to the church and then he took me to the bank to open up a checking account with the rest. It was all part of the learning experience.

When it was time to order nuts for the next year, I had to decide how many I thought I could sell. This was critical. My first year I had ordered and sold thirty-six pounds of pecans, so the next year I decided to order about twice as many. This turned out to be just the beginning of my exponential growth: By the time I "retired" I was nineteen and selling about six hundred pounds of pecans a year.

That first year, I kept track of who bought my pecans; that way I knew to go back to the same people. Word of mouth had also started to spread. I'd go to one house and the customer would say, "Oh, I think my neighbor wants some of these too." And I'd just keep going around knocking on doors, like a guy selling vacuums.

Slowly, my system got much more sophisticated. Selling the nuts took less and less time and I made more and more money. It was so successful that I was making several thousand dollars a year. In 1965, when I was fifteen, I made about three thousand dollars in six weeks.

By my third year I knew I could handle more customers, so I was always on the lookout. One day I noticed the church directory sitting by the phone in my parents' room and I thought, "Well, this is a good group of people to contact, because they all know me from Sunday school." And that was how I started my first mailing list. Eventually I would find any list of any organization that my parents were involved with and send my cards to these people. My mother wasn't sure that was okay, but my father didn't have any problem with it.

A couple years later, the business really broke open with a new technology (technology being a relative term, of course). I found a hand mimeograph machine that I could use to print three-by-five postcards. I used all my nut money from the first few years to buy the machine and it turned out to be a great investment.

I printed tons of little order forms that I would mail to people and they would mail back to me with their orders. At that point, it became almost embarrassingly easy because I didn't even have to go door to door anymore. To this day, it was the easiest money I ever made, by far.

I started buying the best Christmas presents any kid has

ever bought, because money was not an issue. I bought my
parents the most beautiful waffle maker; I think I spent thirty-
five bucks on it. My mother just had a fit that I spent so much
money, but they kept it.

When it came time for me to move to Ohio for college, I
carried the business with me. I ran the business from Ohio,
sending out the order cards and everything, and then I flew
home to New York to do the deliveries. At that point I had it
down to just one pre-Thanksgiving delivery and one pre-
Christmas delivery. I would fly back for the day, deliver the
nuts, and then fly back to college. It sounds crazy, but it was
always worth the investment.

During my junior year, I decided to study abroad in Eu-
rope for the whole year so I tried to sell the nut business. I
used all my church connections to try to find another young
guy who would want to take it over. I thought surely someone would want it; it was such easy money. But I couldn't
find anyone to buy it. I got really concerned because I had
these customers who counted on me, so I tried to *give* the business away. And still, nobody was interested. I couldn't find
a single person. So the business just died. To this day, there
are probably people in my hometown who are upset about
it; they really counted on me.

It's funny because nowadays everyone wants their kids
to be entrepreneurs, and people talk all the time about cash
and earning and investments. When I was growing up we
didn't talk about those sorts of things. We played Little League
and went to Cub Scouts . . . there was just no emphasis on

making money. I don't think anyone at the time knew how well my pecan business was doing.

When my wife and I got married in college we bought our first car and put a down payment on our first house with my savings from those pecans. When I left the business I remember my dad saying, "You could become the nut man! You could make this a real business!" It was just a joke, but he was probably right.

—CHUCK TURNER, *sixty-four, is the associate vice president for development and director of medical development at Yale University.*

The Aluminum Heir

1970

Working at my father's aluminum company was always on my radar, probably because my father was constantly banging the idea into my head. He started the company when I was young and he made it very clear, almost from day one, that he wanted his son to go and work for him.

At first my friends and I just worked in the warehouse on weekends when we were in high school. We were called "squirrels," which pretty much summed up how helpful we were. I would get a call on a Thursday from this guy Frank who was the warehouse manager. He'd say, "Hello, sir, I need three of your squirrel friends on Saturday." So I would be able to decide which of my friends were going to make twenty bucks that weekend. I'd put a crew together and show up. We didn't do much of anything productive; we basically just built skids and swept floors and wadded up newspapers and taped them into balls and drove around in forklift trucks throwing the balls at each other.

This went on throughout high school, until I was accepted into college. Right before I left for school my father and I went up to visit a relative who had been shot in Vietnam and was recovering in a hospital nearby. We're sitting at the foot of this guy's bed and he says, "So, Mike, what are you fuckin' doing with your life?" And I go, "Um, well, I'm going to college next fall." And he goes, "Well, you know what, if you don't have the best fuckin' time of your fuckin' life you've really fucked up."

My dad, who is sitting across the bed from me, looks at me and says, "You know, he's got a point." And I said, "What? Dad, are you telling me to go to college and just have a good time?" And he says, "Well, it didn't hurt me!" So I did go to college and I did have a *very* good time, which basically ruled out being a lawyer or a doctor. I think it was all part of my dad's master plan to make sure I had to work for him . . . But that's just a theory I'm working on.

It was the middle of my sophomore year at college that I finally told my dad I'd go work for him after I graduated. He seemed happy and really relieved, but then he had a heart attack the next month, so maybe he was actually stressed about it. After all, it's not like I had any experience. But when I finished my junior year early and had six months off, my dad put me right to work.

I started back in the warehouse. On my first day the warehouse manager gave me a hacksaw and a metal bar and said, "Cut this bar in half." It was a stainless-steel bar, which is pretty much impossible to cut through, but of course I didn't ask any questions. It took me all day, but I did it, and at the end of the day I handed those two halves to him and said, "Here you go." Everyone was snickering at me because it was a totally pointless task, but I did what I was told and that was a good start.

Shortly after that I got moved into sales. We were selling architectural metals and I didn't really know the product line at all, but I got put on the phones right away. Every call I got made me really, really nervous. The hold button was my best friend. Someone would ask me a question and I'd say, "Yes, hold please" and then I'd shout, "Help!! This guy just asked me a question!"

I had to work the phones for a couple of months and then they put me on outside sales. I would drive my station wagon into the city of Chicago, where most of our accounts were, and I'd try to make a sale. But first I'd drive past the potential customer's office, just to check it out. Then I'd drive around the block . . . and drive around the block again . . . and drive around the block again . . . I was just incredibly nervous, and it would take forever to get my moxie up to go in the door.

I remember the first order I ever got. I walked into this office that had placed orders with us in the past and said, "Hi, I'm Mike Petersen from Petersen Aluminum and I'd like to talk to you about your metal." And the guy goes, "Oh, hey Mike, we were just about to order some metal!" And I said, "Oh . . . well . . . would you like our phone number?" The guy goes, "Well, what are you here for?" and I said, "Oh, right . . . Great!" I'll never forget that. We all laughed about it, but in the end I actually did get the order. It was my first order, I remember it very well. My takeaway from that is that people actually want to see you succeed. Even if you're a real greenie, people want to make life comfortable for you, at least out here in the Midwest.

As I was learning more and more about the business, my dad had several more heart attacks. The more heart attacks he had, the more ornery he became. He started spending more time away from the office, and more time down in Florida. One time when he was away there was a document that needed to be signed. It was an urgent situation, and he was the only one who had the authority to sign the document. It was a disaster.

When he came back from the trip, I had a little speech prepared. It was something like, "Dad, we all want to encourage you to spend time away because Lord knows you've earned it, but I think you should probably consider naming one of us—and I have my own ideas of who it might be—an officer in the company. What do you think?" His response was "Get outta my office!"

About two weeks later my dad said, "I solved our problem," and handed me a stack of business cards that said, "Michael Petersen. Summer Vice President & Winter President." At this point I was very confused, so he said, "That's my answer. In the summer you're vice president. And in the winter, when I'm away, you're president." So I had to give it to him—that was pretty unique.

—MIKE PETERSEN, *sixty, is now the CEO of Petersen Aluminum Corporation during every season. When he started, the annual sales were approximately $5 million; they are now more than $100 million.*

The Striving Shoeshiner

1959

I've been working since I was six years old. My father didn't live with us and I had a very stormy relationship with him, but I remember him talking about how he worked his whole life and how he sold gum on corners in Mexico City when he was my age. That's how I got the notion early on that I could work on my own too, and make a little money.

I first started shining shoes the summer after kindergarten. I lived in a neighborhood called City Terrace, which was about five miles from downtown LA. I would take the bus downtown with my mom, or sometimes by myself because it was the era when you could do that. I shined shoes on Seventh and Broadway. I remember the corner distinctly because it was close to where all the major department stores were, like May Company and Bullock's. I liked that corner because there were affluent people going to those department stores, so there were plenty of men in suits and ties. Sometimes their shoes were already shiny but they wanted me to shine them anyway. I guess they felt sorry for me, who knows.

I was fairly aggressive at hawking my little business so I did pretty well for myself. But the bigger, older shoeshine boys would come from time to time and tell me to leave. They'd move me themselves if I didn't get out fast enough, so I knew when it was time for me to go. I'd have to go over to Fifth and Broadway, where there was a Newberry's five-and-dime store. It was less lucrative because the people who shopped at Newberry's didn't get their shoes shined as regularly, or they didn't wear the types of shoes that needed to be shined. So whenever I got kicked over there I had to be particularly aggressive. I'd stop someone and say, "Come on, sir, let me shine your shoes. Your shoes are so dirty!"

I remember how nice people were, and how they would marvel at such a young kid shining shoes. Often they would give me a pat on the head and ask me how much I had made that day. I think I was charging a quarter for a shine, but, from time to time, people would give me a tip. I knew I couldn't charge much because that was how I got my market share, by charging less than the older shoeshiners.

Then when I was about seven or eight years old, I got a Sunday paper route. The papers got delivered to me around four or five in the morning. It took me an hour to wrap them up and get them on my bike, then it would take a few hours to deliver them. The Sunday papers were so heavy, filled with advertisements and extra pages, and this wasn't your ordinary paper route: I lived at the bottom of a hill, so by the time I loaded my bike up with newspapers, I couldn't even ride up it. I literally had to walk my bike through most of my delivery route. Plus, it was a poor neighborhood so not everyone got the paper. Instead of having twenty homes per block I might have just two homes per block, which meant I could walk a long way and still have a full load of papers. Delivering those newspapers would take five or six hours on a Sunday.

As I grew older I started to take every job I could get. I sold *La Opinion* newspapers outside of fight nights at the Olympic Auditorium when I was nine. I washed dishes. I worked at a bookstore. When I started going to Catholic school I worked as a janitor there. I pulled weeds on the freeway. I cut lawns. I worked at Safeway.

I also worked at pretty much every shop in my neighborhood. There were only a few businesses on City Terrace Drive: a liquor store, a drugstore, a hardware store, a restaurant, and a few markets. I would knock on every door and ask them if they had any work. Everyone said no, because I wasn't fifteen yet and I didn't have a work permit. But I would keep on coming back. And finally I would say, "You don't have to pay me, just let me sweep the floor, let me cut your boxes, let me take out the trash. It won't cost you!" Of course, I said they didn't have to pay me, but I knew they would give me something after it was all done.

This kind of hustle gave me a work ethic, a willingness to knock on doors and not be afraid of getting no for an answer. It also gave me hope that a smile and a bit of confidence could always get you a few dollars. I was never afraid to work.

In fact, I liked to work. In many ways I defined myself by my work. I was always proud that I was never wanting for a job.

When I became the mayor of Los Angeles I was big on summer youth jobs for a lot of reasons. I think it's really important to give kids that experience because of everything I learned about working as a young boy. I also could see it from the perspective of my mother: She liked it when I worked because if I was working I wasn't getting into trouble. My work ethic has always been something that people talk about, and I know that, for me, it had a lot to do with starting off as a young entrepreneur and doing whatever it takes to get a job.

—ANTONIO VILLARAIGOSA, *sixty-two, was the mayor of Los Angeles from 2005 to 2013.*

The Farm-Stand Prodigy

1959

My dad was a farmer in Florida his whole life and he always
had a rough time. Hurricanes, frost, whatever it was, he never
made money farming. In the summer of 1959 he was dead
broke and nothing was selling. He picked his first harvest of
cucumbers, brought 'em into the broker, and was hoping to
have 'em sold for a little money. But they didn't sell. So the
broker was going to dump 'em and he said, "No, I'll come get
my cucumbers."

These cucumbers were in good shape but they couldn't
be shipped because they'd been in the cooler for too long.
The next day Saturday, so he put me, a first-grader, out on
the street corner with a few bushels of 'em and a field crate
and a piece of plywood. I sat there all day long and no one
stopped. My dad figured that it was because no one saw me
there, so the next day he put me out in the same place, this

time with two handwritten signs next to me that simply said, "Robert Is Here." I sold out by noon and walked home. And that was the beginning.

After that first day we started selling cucumbers every weekend, on that same stretch of road and with those same signs. When school let out for Christmas break I worked the whole time. I'd come out every day. After that my mom would set up the stand while I was in school and leave a coffee cup for people to put money in if they took some produce. I'd get off the bus and grab the money and take care of any more customers.

I was nine when I hired my first employee. I wanted someone to work at the stand while I was at school so that we could have it manned at all times instead of using the honor system. My mom and dad were working on the farm during the day so we hired a neighbor lady. Her husband had died of a heart attack on his tractor, so she needed to work to pay her bills. She helped us and we helped her. She worked for me for a very long time—it was like having your grandmother take care of your business for you.

My family all worked together, you know. If I needed help at the stand, someone would help me, and if they needed help on the farm, I helped on the farm too. Everyone worked to put money in the pot so we could buy food and whatever we needed for the house. Mom put some money away for me after we started making a little bit, but to start with it was just all so we could keep going.

My dad was not a role model—just the opposite. He was abusive to my mom, abusive to my brothers and myself. He was always the adversary. My mom, on the other hand, was completely different. She was the hardest-working person I knew, and put up with more crap and withstood more than anyone I'd ever seen.

When I was fourteen I bought ten acres of land and a house. Matter of fact, I still own that land and someone is out there picking mangos on it right now. In 1978, about twenty years after I sold my first cucumber on the side of the road, I built the building where my fruit stand is now. We were just gettin' too busy in the old place, so I built a new structure right behind it. Now we have animals, live music, milkshakes, all that. But yeah, it is in the same place as my very first stand. Why would I move?

And no, I never thought of using another name, not at all. We're still called Robert Is Here. Colonel Sanders didn't change his sign. What we are is what we are. Robert Is Here is weird enough to really catch the eye. It's completely unorthodox. It doesn't tell you what I do; it does tell you where I am. I don't really play with the computer, but I know that no matter where you are in the world, you put "Robert Is Here" into the computer and it'll tell you how to get here. That's pretty bizarre.

I have four kids now. They've all gone to college and then they've all come back to the farm. I couldn't run the farm stand without the family; I'd have to get rid of it. Business was going pretty good until Hurricane Andrew hit in 1992 and destroyed everything I had built and grown. My farm, my barn, my house . . . everything, just completely destroyed. I was left with no income and no money. I had to sell twenty-five acres of land, but we rebuilt. Once a farmer, always a farmer. It's just what we do.

—ROBERT MOEHLING, *sixty-one, owns fifty-five acres of land and a popular fruit stand near Everglades National Park in Florida that is considered a tourist attraction. A large sign above the stand reads "Robert Is Here" in tall letters.*

The Wienermobile Driver

2006

Right now I live and work in Manhattan, where everyone dresses up and is really chic all the time, so when people find out I used to drive the Wienermobile they are usually like, "What?!" I grew up in Yonkers, and so the first time I had ever even heard of the Wienermobile—which is a Midwestern phenomenon—was when they came to recruit at my college, Penn State. I saw this gigantic hot dog on wheels, and then these two cute, petite girls hopped out of it. I was like, "Is this even serious?"

But when they started telling us about the job I thought it might actually be cool. The recruiter said that Wienermobile drivers, who were officially called "Hotdoggers," were basically spokespeople for a major corporation. They pitched media, set up press materials, and did interviews. Then, at the end of the day, they are able to say that they worked for a major corporation for a year. I was majoring in PR and I didn't have any experience so I thought I should at least consider it.

I applied and, after a surprisingly rigorous interview process, I got the job. I signed a one-year contract, was paired up with another Hotdogger, and was assigned a Midwestern region. Our job was basically to drive all over the Midwest, sleep in hotels every night, and talk with people about Oscar Mayer as a brand. I could only go home for Thanksgiving, Christmas, and a little spring break that year. I had never been away from home for that long.

In the Midwest, pretty much everyone knew what the Wienermobile was. They had grown up with it, they had seen it drive down the street, or they had at least heard of it. That was great because when someone is not familiar with the Wienermobile, the first thing they ask is, "What the heck is this?" and the second thing they ask is, "Could I have a hot dog?" Then I had to explain to them, "I'm sorry, we don't have hot dogs, but we have Wienerwhistles."

Wienerwhistles are what Oscar Mayer came up with as a fun little takeaway from the Wienermobile. They are tiny Wienermobile-shaped whistles. They've been handing them out since forever. I would meet people who were seventy or eighty years old who would come up and say, "I saw this when I was nine years old and I got a Wienerwhistle." Other people who had never heard of the Wienerwhistle before didn't know the nostalgia behind it; maybe they thought it was stupid. They would be the ones who would say, "But I really just want a hot dog."

Almost everyone got excited to look inside the Wiener-mobile, just because it looked so crazy on the outside. And it was pretty cool on the inside, too: The floor was a reddish hot dog color with a streak of mustard in the middle and the ceiling was painted to look like the sky. There were six seats in it. Sometimes people would win a local contest and their prize was a ride in the Wienermobile. They always loved it.

The thing you have to get used to really fast, almost from day one, is that when you're in the Wienermobile everyone is honking at you, everyone is taking pictures of it, every-one is waving at you, and you have to wave back, honk back, and just always have a smile on your face. The Wienermo-bile was also our only car. So, sure we got two days off a week, but if we wanted to go to the mall or the movies or some-thing, we had to drive the Wienermobile! It was crazy.

That got rough when our day was over and we would go to get a nice dinner and, right when we're about to cut into a big steak or something, people would come up and be like, "Hi, I'd really like to see the inside of the Wienermobile right now." And you're like, "Okay, when I'm done eating I can show it to you." And they're like, "No, I have to leave soon, I want to see it now." And what can you do? You're the face of the brand in that moment, so you have to be friendly and accommodating. I remember once I ran into Target after a re-ally long event and I'm looking through a rack, and I hear this woman on the other side go, "I don't know where those Wienermobile people are but we're going to *find* them, and we're going to *make* them show it to us!" I seriously felt like I was being hunted. I pulled a sweater off the rack and I put it on to cover the Wienermobile logo on my shirt and I was like, "Oh my God, please don't let her figure me out!" It got to the point where, if it was our day off, we would park the Wienermobile at one end of the parking lot and literally *run* away from it so no one knew it was ours. That was one of the biggest lifestyle changes, honestly. Driving the Wiener-mobile makes you feel like you're some sort of celebrity.

Traveling all over the Midwest was a bit of a culture shock for me. I mean, we have farmland in New York, like upstate, but it has a beginning and an end. In the Midwest you can just drive forever and ever without ever seeing a stoplight or a town with more than eight hundred people in it. But the Midwest was also where I saw some amazing things, like the world's largest ball of twine, or a cow carved out of butter. It blew my mind.

This job was also my first experience with Midwestern kindness. For example, one woman I met at that state fair found out that I hadn't been home in months and that I had been eating only fast food. She was so horrified that, the next day, she brought me a Tupperware full of home-cooked food. A complete dinner, right down to a mini pie. I was so touched!

A lot of times we would leave the Wienermobile in a park-ing lot somewhere and people would leave notes on the windshield like, "Come to our son's 5th birthday party at this address!" We'd try to fulfill it if we could. We got one once that was from a facility for hearing-impaired children. The note said that it was a really small facility but the kids would love to see the Wienermobile, so we said, "Let's go!"

As it turns out the kids, who were all five or six years old, had recently gotten cochlear implants so they could hear, and the facility was working with them on their speech. The teacher lined up the kids and they got inside the Wienermobile and we gave them all whistles. When they got the whistles they all looked at them like, "What the heck is this?" And the teacher showed them how to blow into it, and they were all kind of startled. It was the first time the majority of them had ever heard a whistle, and they were just so happy to hear it, they were so delighted by that noise. They were crawling all over the inside of the Wienermobile and communicating in a jumble of sign language and speech. I just felt like, you know what, this is why I have this job. This is the point. It's a nice surprise for people and they are just never going to forget it. That was one of my favorite days.

I realized later that, the year I got the Wienermobile gig, almost two thousand people had applied, and they only picked twelve. And afterward, basically everything those recruiters said came true: I had this amazing experience on the road, I went to so many places I had never been to and probably will never have a reason to go back to, and, afterward, I interviewed with every major PR firm in the city and got a job almost immediately.

—NATASHA BEST, *thirty, is an account supervisor at a large PR firm in New York City. She has worked with major clients such as Procter & Gamble and Gallo wines. She still enjoys a good Oscar Mayer hot dog.*

The Survivor-
Camp Staffer

2014

When I was four years old, the deep fryer in the back of my family's gas station caught on fire and exploded. I was badly burned. I read that every day you spend in the hospital after a burn injury represents about 1 percent of your body that's been burned. I was in the hospital for a month.

My burn was really severe because I was so young. They didn't think that I would survive because I had inhaled a lot of smoke and my internal organs were swollen from all the heat. I was in a coma for about two weeks.

My recovery took a long time and every time my mom and I would go for my checkups or to get my bandages redone, the doctors would hand us a brochure from the Alisa Ann Ruch Burn Foundation's Champ Camp and say, "You should really go to this." My mom was hesitant because I was so young, but when I was nine years old she finally let me go.

Champ Camp is a weeklong camp for young burn survivors. There's a medical staff on site for kids who are still in treatment, but other than that it's a really classic camp. There are cabins and all sorts of activities like archery, horseback riding, and water slides.

My favorite activity at camp was people watching. I have always been really, really shy. I don't know if that comes from being a burn survivor or if it's because I'm from a pretty conservative Asian family, but even when I was a young camper I liked sitting in the background and watching the transitions that kids made at camp.

This camp is in the Central Valley where it can be over a hundred degrees in the summer, and some young girls would wear sweaters all day. Wearing a sweater in the middle of summer is pretty inconvenient, so everyone else was really aware of the fact that they were wearing sweaters and that they were probably doing it to cover their burns. But then, at some point during the camp, no one would say anything, but everyone could see that they were becoming more comfortable with themselves. Even as a camper I noticed these cool changes that would happen in kids.

Now that I'm older I really don't care when people stare at my burns. Whatever. But I think a part of that is because I was able to let my guard down at a camp where everyone else had been through the same thing. I saw that I was really just like any other kid and that I could have just as much fun.

When I turned sixteen I was too old to be a camper, but not old enough to be a full counselor, so my advisers recommended me to be a counselor in training, or CIT. I was pretty unsure of myself as a CIT because, although I've always been a responsible kid, I'm also very quiet, which doesn't always make for the best counselor. You want your counselor to be kind of crazy and outgoing and I was worried that I wouldn't be able to help my campers have a good time.

I learned very quickly that summer how easy it is to make sure kids have a good time at camp. I have a particularly strong memory of riding in the go-karts with a girl who had been injured so badly by her burns that she was in a wheelchair, but when I was driving her around in the go-kart she was laughing like absolutely nothing was wrong. To hear her laughter and know that she was laughing because of something I was doing was pretty awesome.

When I turned twenty I was too old to be a CIT anymore. Not everyone that's a CIT becomes a full counselor, sometimes they ask you to mature a bit more before you can come back and work. So that summer when I was twenty I had no idea what would happen to me, and I cried so much on the last day of camp. Every year that I skipped camp had always been a really difficult year for me, so I felt like, if I couldn't go to camp next summer, it had the potential to ruin my whole year. Then, in January, I got a call from the new camp director who asked me to join the program, not as a counselor but as a staff. I was so excited.

My job on staff was to schedule all the campers for their activities each day. There are over a hundred kids at this camp, so I'd stay up until two o'clock in the morning some nights trying to figure out who should go where and when. It's like a giant puzzle because you don't want to schedule anyone too much for one activity, but you want people to be doing activities all day.

During the day I tried to play with the kids when I could, but the scheduling was a full commitment. I worked in the back office so I didn't get much interaction with the campers at all; I would just hear stories from other counselors about their campers and how they were progressing.

At first I was pretty bummed that I wasn't a direct influence on the kids. I kept hearing about one particular girl who had been in a pretty serious burn accident. I had met her the first day at camp and she was incredibly shy. But when I saw her at the end of the week, all of that had changed. She was laughing and having the time of her life and it made me realize how, even though I was working behind the scenes, I really gave every single kid such an amazing experience. It felt really cool to have that responsibility.

The toughest part of being on staff is the end of the week when we send off all the campers. We form two lines to create an aisle that the kids walk through as they board the bus and we hug every single camper. When you hug good-bye as a camper it's already really sad, but when you're on staff, it's just heartbreaking. You're seeing all these kids crying because they don't want to go home and all you can think is, "I don't want you to go home either!" The first time I did this I was surprised by how hard it was to say good-bye to the campers. I told one of my old counselors I felt this way and she said, "Oh, and it gets harder every year."

Early on in my CIT days, one of my favorite counselors told me that she didn't accept a job promotion because she wouldn't get the vacation time during camp. At the time I was like, "Wow, that's a pretty intense commitment." But now I'm in New York City looking for a job and I always find myself worrying, "What if I get a full-time job and I can't go to camp next year?" So I guess that means I see myself being a part of this camp for a really, really long time.

—CHRISTINA MIN, *twenty-two, graduated from the University of California, Santa Barbara, with a bachelor of arts in sociology in 2014. She's an intern on the Alisa Ann Ruch Burn Foundation board. For more information on Champ Camp visit aarbf.org.*

WHEN IT COULDN'T GET WORSE

The Horror Stories

The Alaskan Adventure

2003

The summer before my senior year my best friend Dan and I went camping on the San Juan Islands for eight days. We were seventeen years old and it was our first trip without an adult. We loved it. So senior year, as we were getting ready to graduate and go off to different colleges, Dan and I wanted to do something bigger and better. We wanted to go camping and hiking in Alaska—it was the most adventurous place we could imagine—but we didn't have enough money to travel there from our hometown in Oregon. Then Dan's sister saw an ad in the "Wanted" section of the local newspaper for a job at a salmon processing plant in Alaska that included transportation up there. We figured we could get paid to go for a few weeks, work a bit, then go exploring. Basically a free trip to Alaska, right?

The job interview was at the unemployment center in

downtown Portland. We were by far the youngest people
there and it wasn't so much an "interview" as it was a chance
for the interviewer to convince us that the job wasn't going
to be that bad and persuade us that we might even enjoy it.
There weren't many questions for me and it was certainly not
based on whether or not I was qualified.

What sold us was the financial arrangement: The hourly
wage was great and the company would pay for half of your
airfare up there, and after you had successfully completed
your stint, they would reimburse you for the other half
and buy your flight home. The trip to Alaska was long and
expensive—it involved a commercial flight to Anchorage; a
separate small, chartered flight; and then a two-hour bus
ride to Naknek, which is right near Bristol Bay. It's a remote,
beautiful place; the perfect spot to start an adventure.

We both had a month free that summer, so our plan was
to go up to Alaska on the company's dime, work two weeks
during peak season, then head out into the wilderness. In the
interview, everyone acted like that plan was totally cool, no
problem. But once we got up there, that wasn't really the case.

When we arrived at the processing plant in Naknek we
started exploring the town. That didn't take long. There was
a grocery store, a bar, a post office, and a liquor store. That
was it. No traffic lights, which was fine because there wasn't
much traffic. The town itself has fewer than a thousand people
who lived there permanently. And even though I was imag-
ining a dramatic, mountainous landscape, Naknek is on a
tundra so it was just a lot of flat, spongy ground.

When we got back to the plant we had some training and

then we waited. There was a lot of waiting around when we first got up there, because the salmon run had started late. We didn't have much to do until the salmon started swimming upstream. Then finally, on the third day, the salmon came. There were just so many, all at once. I had never seen anything like it. As soon as the fish came in, we were working full throttle: Our shift was from 6:00 a.m. to 10:00 p.m. every day. That means that we only had eight hours a day where we weren't on the clock. No days off.

The process worked like this: When the fish arrived at the plant from the boat they were placed on a conveyor belt and immediately run through a machine that cuts off their heads. Then they go through the "slime line," where workers cleaned the fish and pulled out the guts. This was the messiest job. The salmon were then placed on large metal trays that were stacked a dozen high; this was called a rack. That rack was rolled into a flash freezer that was about forty degrees below zero. The fish would freeze so fast that they would freeze to the trays and the trays would freeze to the rack and the rack would freeze to the floor.

The next station was "case up," which was where I worked. We put the fish in cases for shipping. The first step was breaking the fish off the rack. Each tray weighed about fifty pounds and we'd have to lift it above our heads and then slam it down onto a wide table to loosen the frozen fish from the tray. Then we'd rinse off the fish, put them into bags and put the bags into boxes. Finally, we put the boxes onto pallets and they were shipped away.

We'd all rotate because breaking racks was incredibly

tiring. The facility was kept really cold but whoever was breaking racks would be covered in sweat and have steam rising from their body. I think that the most you could possibly do would be a two-hour shift breaking racks. So after you spent a couple of hours on it, you'd go do something else that was easier on your body.

After two weeks, Dan and I were exhausted. There was a whiteboard near the cafeteria and every day the boss would write the names of people from the plant who were being discharged and getting their ticket to leave. As soon as two weeks had passed, we checked to see if our names were on there. They weren't. We started checking every day. Still nothing.

We quickly realized that we couldn't leave until someone else decided it was time. The whole reason we were there in the first place was because we didn't have any money to travel, so we were kind of stuck. We literally could not afford to leave without the company paying for it. I had a brief period of despair. I felt that I didn't know what I had gotten myself into. The only thing I wanted to do was leave, but I couldn't.

As time went on, people started to get edgy and their tempers got shorter. One guy started talking a lot about "psychological warfare" and launching "psychological attacks" on people. On payday it was especially bad because people would spend their entire paychecks at the bar. It got crazy. One guy took a hammer to a big metal staircase in the middle of the night because he was so fed up. The next morning, someone on the slime line came in completely drunk. He picked up two salmon by the tails, one in each hand, and started waving them around over his head, screaming, "Don't come near me!" He was wasted and fed up. He was quitting in style.

As things were getting worse and worse, the boss kept straight-up lying to Dan and me over and over again about when we were getting out of there. We were complaining as much as we could. We didn't complain about the work, but we would say to him, "You told us we could leave after two weeks of work. Our time is running out." He kept saying, "Don't worry about it, it will be tomorrow!" or "Check back with me in two days," or "I know I said it would be today but something came up and I can't lose you guys yet. Check back tomorrow." But since they were paying for our flight home, if we had chosen to leave before they discharged us we would have walked away with nothing—it would have taken our entire pay to travel back home. So that really wasn't an option.

On July 17, exactly a month after we got there, our names finally appeared on the whiteboard. I still remember the date. When we saw them we were literally jumping for joy, hugging each other. We were just so happy. To this day it is still, honestly, one of the happiest moments of my life. We flew out just hours after that. We went straight to the airport. I guess we never got our Alaskan adventure . . . at least not the one we imagined.

—EVAN MCKITTRICK, *twenty-nine, heads Teach For America's national service and engagement initiative as a director of strategic initiatives and partnerships. He has not returned to Alaska.*

The Water Park Janitor

2004

I grew up a few miles away from a huge water park—the biggest amusement park in the area. I'd go there a couple of times every summer, but it was a little pricey for my family—it cost about fifteen dollars per person to get in at the time. I always wanted to have my birthday party there when I was little but my mom said it was too expensive so I never did. Looking back, that was really for the best.

When I turned fifteen I got my worker's permit, then went straight to the water park to apply for a job. It was a little late in the hiring season, so they only had one position open—park attendant. It sounded totally cool and like a really respectable job. I thought it would be something like park ranger, you know? So I took it. Turns out "park attendant" is just another way to say "janitor."

The park had two giant slides, a couple different play

pools, a lazy river ride . . . It was a really big attraction. Hundreds of people came every day, and my main job was to keep the bathrooms clean, empty the trash, and take care of any messes on the deck. Once I was working behind the scenes, I saw what a filthy place it really was. The lazy river was always filled with trash or condoms, and the pools constantly had to be shut down because a diaper filled with poop would be floating around in it or something.

The bathrooms were a really dirty job. One time I had to clean up human shit on the floor. I like to think it was an accident by some little kid, but you never know. You just can't forget a thing like that! But I think the worst part was taking out the trash. The trash bags were always crawling with maggots, and we'd have to take them out right past everyone who was eating at the food court. It was humiliating. People were disgusted; they'd jump away from you. Meanwhile, you were trying to swat away flies, make sure the bag didn't break open, and keep your polo shirt from getting trash juice all over it.

The problem with the cleaning system was that it was run by teenagers, so it was a little . . . disorganized. We had piles for clean rags and dirty rags, but people would constantly use a rag to clean the bathroom and then take it to wipe down the tables at the food court. Disgusting, right?

I got pretty fed up with all the gross people who went to this park. One time a guy leaned out of the pool, vomited on the deck, looked at me, and said, "You have to clean this up," and then just swam away. I thought to myself, "I can clean this up right, or I could just do it the easy way." So I got a hose out and just rinsed it off the deck, back into the pool. Oops.

I earned $5.15 an hour. The girls earned $5.25. How that worked, I have no idea. I used it all as spending money. My mom worked part-time at Costco and part-time as a house cleaner so she could buy me what I needed. But there were certain things I just *wanted*. I bought my first cell phone with that money—a flip phone from Verizon. I didn't save a cent that summer.

I had friends who went back summer after summer and eventually became managers, but that life was not for me. I loved earning my own money and having an income, but I knew that I would need something better in the long term. I think it was really my first lesson in the importance of an education.

—W., *twenty-five, is an environmental and sustainability studies major at a university near his hometown. He still jogs around the water park when he goes for runs, but does not visit anymore.*

The Bacon Packer

1972

The summer after my first year of college my friends and I would spend all day at the beach. Then I'd go home, change out of my bikini, put a sweater over my sunburn, and go into a refrigerated bacon-packing factory for most of the night. At the time, factories paid better than any other summer job, and the night shift paid the best.

There were two types of people who worked at the bacon-packing factory: the seasonal employees, like me, and the regulars, who worked there year-round. There were also the mechanics who did the heavy lifting, like bringing in the slabs of bacon. They were kind of the young, muscular playboys, checking out all the college girls. Unfortunately, everybody who worked in this place had to wear plastic shower caps over their heads, so it was hard to tell if these guys were actually handsome.

As a factory worker, you could have any job along the line. You could be the person that weighed the bacon, you could be the person that got the slices all organized before they were shrink-wrapped and packaged, or you could be the person that made sure the bacon packs looked right before they went into shipping boxes. I liked being the weigher because you had to have a little experience to do that job; it was sort of a reward for the best workers.

Sometimes when I was at the weighing station, chunks of bacon would get caught in the slicer. Eventually they would fall out, but it would really bother me that this chunk of bacon was just sitting there, kind of jammed in the slicer. I didn't want it to fall out on *my* bacon that I was packaging so beautifully! So, when this happened, I'd just stick my finger in there to loosen it. One time, a longtime supervisor came over said, "What are you doing?" and I said, "Well, there's a chunk of bacon in there and I'm trying to get it out." He held up his hand—he only had three fingers. He said, "This happened to me when I did that." I don't know if that was true, but I never stuck my finger in there again.

I grew up in a pretty blue-collar neighborhood on the South Side of Chicago, but hanging out with full-time factory workers was still pretty new to me. There was one full-time worker who we used to call Diamond Lil because she would come into work every day wearing nice pants and a fancy shirt, and she would wear these long, sparkly earrings that would dangle out of her plastic cap. She was kind of old and cranky but she turned out to be one of my favorite regulars. At the end of the summer she said, "So, you having fun here?"

And I said, "Oh, well, this has been a great job . . ." and she said, "Yeah, but is it *fun*? Is it *fun* for you to be here?" And so I said, "Well, no, it's not really *fun* . . ." and then she said, "Well, then stay in college, get your degree, or you'll end up doing this forever."

—RITA CARBONARI, *fifty-nine, graduated from the University of Illinois. She now works in the development office of a liberal arts college. She claims that bacon is still one of her favorite foods.*

The Undocumented Dreamer

2007

I was born in Mexico, in the state of Guerrero, in a very
rural town that was so small there weren't any paved roads
or even a hospital. It was very agricultural and there was a
lot of poverty. A few years after I was born, we moved to
another town where the biggest employer was a textile factory. My mom got a job making the dress slacks that you
see at big department stores in the United States, but eventually the work began to decrease and people began to lose
their jobs.

That's when my dad decided to go to the United States.
He crossed the border and was in the US for a year before
he sent for my mother, my two brothers, and myself. He
was working in North Carolina and it wasn't easy for him

there but he knew that, for us kids, there were going to be better opportunities there than the ones we had in Mexico.

So, when I was ten years old and my older brother was thirteen and my youngest brother was one year old, we crossed the Arizona desert with my mother and a group of about twelve other people. To cross we had to first take a bus to a border town. I had never been outside the state of Guerrero, or outside of my community really, but on our way to the border we drove by fields of corn and big cities and so many beautiful places. I was staring out the window discovering my country as I was leaving it. It was very beautiful just to get to know Mexico but also very sad because even then I knew I wasn't going to be back.

It took us five days and four nights to cross the desert. The thing I remember the most is my mom carrying my little brother. She was very protective and she wouldn't let anyone else other than us help her carry him. Later she told us that, as we were walking, she saw a human skeleton in the sand. She kept walking and pretended like she didn't see it so that we wouldn't see it. Crossing was terrifying, but it brought us closer as a family.

Finally we made it to Phoenix, Arizona, and from Phoenix we went to North Carolina, where my dad was. Because I was old enough to remember the crossing, I always knew that I was undocumented. I went to elementary school, middle school, and high school here in North Carolina. Other kids got jobs in high school but I never did because I knew I didn't have that nine-digit Social Security number you need to get a job. Instead, I played sports and I went to school, but I didn't want to think about what was going to happen next.

I had never told anyone that I was undocumented, not friends and especially not teachers. But when I was a senior in high school I wanted to know what I could do, what my options were. So I went to my high school counselor for a thirty-minute meeting. We talked about school for a bit and then, five minutes before the meeting was supposed to end, I told her the truth: I was undocumented. I had never told anybody so I didn't know how she was going to react, and I was shaking when I told her. I still remember the words that she told me, exactly. She said, "Oliver, the only opportunity you have is for you to go back where you came from."

Looking back, I can see that that moment could have broken me. But instead, it made me stronger. I've always been very stubborn, and from the moment I heard my counselor say that, I knew inside that I was going to go to school one day and that, no matter what, I was going to make it here.

After I graduated I was able to enroll in a community college, but if you are undocumented in North Carolina you have to pay out-of-state tuition, which was about three times as much as the in-state students had to pay. So at that point I knew that I had to find work. I couldn't rely on my parents because they had other bills to pay. I needed to find a way to earn money on my own.

Of course, in order to get a job, you need to have a Social Security number, which I still did not. But there is a whole underground economy for this that people don't really like to talk about; there are people who can provide you with a Social Security number and a work employment authorization card. They are not valid and this is not legal, of course, but it will usually work, at least for a little bit.

One day I met someone in the parking lot of a Walmart who I heard could help me get a Social Security number. I remember waiting for him and being very afraid that the police were going to come and I was going to be deported. It was a risk, but I knew that I had to find a job and, for now, this was the only way. So I met this stranger in the parking lot, followed him to a place where he took a picture of me for the ID card, and, three hours later, I had my paperwork. It cost $500, a huge amount for me.

As soon as I got that paperwork I immediately started applying for jobs. The first place I applied was a pizza place where my mom knew there were a lot of undocumented workers already, so I wouldn't have any problems. The job was making pizzas, which was very repetitive and not very exciting. It also didn't pay much—it was minimum wage and most of the people who worked there had to have a second job just to survive.

The management knew that we were undocumented, but they pretended like they didn't. Their attitude toward us was, basically, "Don't ever forget that you are completely replaceable." I'd show up for the shift on my schedule but then at the end of it the manager would say, "We're very busy, we need you to stay." And when I said, "No, I have to go to class," they would remind me that there were other people out there that could do my job, that I didn't have any special skills, and that I was totally replaceable, so I might as well stay if I wanted to keep my job.

I worked at that job for a year and a half before I got a better job at a department store in the mall. But, about a year into that job, my manager called me into her office and told me there was something wrong with my Social Security number and that I should go down to the Social Security office to see what was up. She gave me half a day off just to go to see. I knew, of course, that my number was bad and I couldn't do anything, so I just went and had a long lunch that day and then came back in to work. The next day she asked me what had happened and I had to tell her truth. I told her that my Social Security number was not valid because, on paper, I shouldn't be here. I told her that I really liked this job but that I knew she had policies and whatever decision she made, I would accept. She told me that she couldn't have me there. I was fired, not because of my performance or my attitude, but because of a number that I didn't have.

I didn't make any friends at either of these jobs. At the pizza place I was friendly with some of the other Latino workers because I knew we were all in the same situation, but I was wary of making friends with other people because I didn't want them to know I was undocumented. I was afraid something would slip out and they would tell the manager. It felt strange too to blend my social life and my work life, because I knew there were limits to what they could know about me.

For a long time I was really afraid to come out as undocumented, but as I got more involved with the immigrant youth movement I heard more and more people from around the country say, "I am undocumented and unafraid." It took me a while to say that too, but when I finally did it felt so good. I didn't have to hide who I was anymore. Yes, I am undocumented, but that's not my entire identity. I am a student and a brother and all these different things. For someone to just call me "illegal" or "undocumented" and just embody my whole existence in this word, I just don't accept that.

This past summer I finished college and the week I graduated I found out that I had gotten DACA [Deferred Action for Childhood Arrivals], which meant that I got a work permit and a Social Security number for the first time. But, more than that, it made me feel that someone finally recognized that this is my home.

Before getting deferred action I was afraid that, no matter what job I had and how good I was, they could just fire me at any time. But now I go to work at a job that I like and I don't have to worry about being called into the manager's office and being told that it's my last day. That's not a threat for me anymore, but it is bittersweet because so many of my friends and family members are still undocumented. I know that feeling of uncertainty and I know that many people still need relief.

—OLIVER MERINO, *twenty-five, graduated from Johnson C. Smith University and now works as a coordinator at the Levine Museum of the New South. He is also an activist with United We Dream, the largest immigrant-youth-led organization in the country. Learn more at unitedwedream.org.*

The Disillusioned Dishwasher

1974

I got my driver's license when I was sixteen and my dad said, "I'm going to give you my car, but you're going to have to pay for your own insurance and gas." So I was like, "Oh great. Thanks, Dad, that's really nice of you."

I heard about a job at the local bar and restaurant so I went in and applied and that was how I became a dishwasher at K&P's. The restaurant was named after the two owners, Kate and Pete. It was very dark inside and the place was nice in an old-school way, with white tablecloths and a steak-and-seafood menu, that whole thing.

Kate was the spearhead, the real manager. She would supply all the food and deal with the money; she was pretty headstrong. I guess you would call Pete the "silent partner."

He was this pasty white guy who looked like he never saw the sun. Apparently he lived above the restaurant but I never actually saw him go up or down the stairs. He would find a spot in the darkest corner of the bar and just kind of park himself there.

I'd spend my shifts in the kitchen with the cooks. It was a pretty fun gig. I mean, obviously I was cleaning people's slop—that part wasn't so great—but I had my own apron and a little hat, and I would goof around with the older waitresses. They'd give me a hard time and I'd tease them right back, that kind of thing.

Right next to the restaurant was the local grocery store. Kate hated how they would waste food, just throw it out when it wasn't looking fresh enough to sit on the shelves anymore. So one day she grabbed a few heads of lettuce out of the grocery store trash, brought them back into the kitchen, and told me to run them through the dishwasher. I thought that was just nuts! But she wouldn't let up about it so I did, and it actually worked—the lettuce came out clean—but everything there started to seem a little shady after that.

They were paying me a dollar an hour and, after the lettuce incident, I decided I wanted a raise, so I asked Kate for five cents more an hour. I had never been late, never missed a day, but when I asked for that raise Kate said, "No, I don't think we're going to do that." So I got a new job as a dishwasher at another restaurant down the street that paid me more.

Since then, I've told my dad a hundred times that not paying for my gas and car insurance was the best thing he ever did for me. I had a couple friends who didn't have to pay for anything, they just got an allowance from their parents that covered it all, and I think they really missed out on a learning experience.

I made sure that all of my kids worked during high school. What I told my kids is that there's always going to be a boss, and whether you like her or not, she's the boss. Do what you have to do, and if you don't want to do it, then you need to move on. I think that's the kind of stuff that, when you learn it at a young age, helps you run faster in your career. Not because you were a dishwasher, but because you learned at least one aspect of what having a job means.

—JOHN FELTON, *fifty-eight, sells packaging in the biotech industry. He still lives in the California town where he grew up. K&P's is now a dive bar.*

The Atheist Bible Salesman

1960

My father was a physicist, and so I've always had a very literal, nonreligious background. But when I was a junior in college a friend of mine heard about a summer job selling Bibles. We'd get a free trip to Nashville for training, which sounded fun, and then they'd send us to different towns around the country to sell Bibles door-to-door. For some reason, which I don't know now, it seemed like a really great idea.

So we went down to the training in Nashville. I didn't know this at the time, but Nashville is the Bible-publishing capital of the United States, and this training was a huge operation; I was pretty amazed. Most of the other salespeople were about my age, but they were all very religious. The Bible really meant something to them and, for probably half the

people there, selling Bibles was the only way they could
get out and go somewhere that their parents would agree to.
For me, it was just a summer job, so I was a little cynical,
but I wasn't arguing with anybody, I was just trying to get
along.

Once we learned how to fill out all the forms at this training camp, they started trying to teach us to really make some
sales. For the most part, the assumption was that this Bible
is a valuable product. In fact, it's a blessed product, and a lot
of people really think they're doing a service to get this stuff
out there. So I think they were motivated by this idea, that
it's a useful thing to be doing in addition to a way to make
money.

But, of course, the money still had to be made. They
brought in their champion salesman to talk to us. I remember being in a big room when this guy with the flashiest
clothes came in with a huge, funny hat, and talked to us for
what felt like hours about his Cadillac and the secrets to his
success. His sales strategy, it appeared, was basically to impress people and to be the most positive person *ever* because
then people would be attracted to you and they'd want to
buy your Bibles. I guess he was very successful, but the rest
of us didn't feel like we were necessarily attractive and we
certainly didn't have Cadillacs going for us. How could we
ever be like him?

After a week of this they assigned us to our sales regions.
My friend and I were assigned to a town called Wellington,
Missouri, which was forty miles to the east of Kansas City.

Wellington was one of a few small towns on the Missouri River, and it was corn-growing country out there. That's what people did and, in the 1960s, it wasn't too mechanized; there were still people who went behind the plow with a horse pulling it and all that. We got a room in some lady's apartment and introduced ourselves as the new Bible salesmen. That was a role that the people in the town understood; they had had Bible salesmen around before. I think the pastor was a little, well, less than happy to see us because he was the one who usually sold the Bibles and made a little cash of his own that way.

But my friend and I immediately got started knocking on doors. I have this picture in my mind of driving up a long driveway with potholes in it and getting to a worn-out house and people sitting on the front porch rocking. It might have been my first sales call or my last; they all kind of blended together after a while.

My sales pitch was very sincere. Because I knew I wasn't going to be able to tell them anything about religion, I decided I was just going to tell them about our range of product, like I was selling anything else. We had a very cheap Bible that was about a dollar, so I'd start with that and then I'd work my way up to the twenty-five-dollar gilded Bible, which was completely covered with gold leaf and had a big place in the front for you to write in family events like the birth of a child. The idea of the gilded Bible was that it would last through generations, so I told people that if they could afford this Bible, it would be a nice thing for their children.

I would pretty much stop there, because that was about as honest as I could get. To me, that Bible would never be worth it, but it might have been to them. That was their decision.

Sales is hard, but it's even harder if you don't believe in your product. It's not like I was going around recruiting people for peace or environmental issues. If religion ever came up I would slide out of the conversation immediately. It just wasn't something I wanted to engage with. Those people respected the Bible and they respected the Bible salesmen almost as religious figures, but I wasn't really bringing that message to them so well.

At night my friend and I would secretly drive to other towns and buy a six-pack of beer and go to the drive-in movie, because we, as Bible salesmen, couldn't ever be seen drinking in our town. We were there maybe a month total, and I went to the drive-in more times that month than I had in my entire life.

The thing that began to get to me, even more than not being able to buy a drink in town, was that our role was really to extract money from these poor people, and it seemed a lot like exploitation. They had these hugely difficult lives working on the farm, lives that were harder and more physically demanding than the lives of anyone else that I knew, and here I was trying to take some money off of them.

Eventually I just—well, I couldn't do it anymore, and the same thing happened to my buddy. So after about a month we wound up going to Chicago with our tails between our legs and no money because we had been working on commission and, needless to say, didn't sell much. We spent the rest of the summer painting houses in Illinois.

—BOB ELLIS, *seventy-four, is a retired data-processing architect in the Bay Area.*

The Zoo Chef

2002

When I was a kid, I really, really, *really* wanted to become a zookeeper. I was obsessed with the idea and I was certain that it was what I wanted to do for the rest of my life. I never actually became a zookeeper—I was taught that Noah's flood created the Grand Canyon, so there was no way in hell I was ever going to pass a biology course, but that's a different story.

So anyway, my dream was to become a zookeeper. As luck would have it, Wichita, Kansas, where I grew up, had a world-class zoo. It was a beautiful zoo that had tons of money pouring in from big corporations, and it showed. I went there at least once a month.

When I was fourteen I applied for their Zoo Crew program. This program basically let kids follow zookeepers around on the weekends and do their grunt work. I loved it.

Our primary tasks revolved around animal excrement. We'd shovel elephant poop into wheelbarrows and dump it out into a truck, over and over again. We'd go see the tapirs, these adorable little elephant-rhinoceros hybrids, and scoop the tapir poop out of the fake river in their exhibit. I got to learn the different consistencies of animal poop during those weekends. Like, elephant poop is pretty solid, but tapir poop is really runny. I'll never forget that.

The Zoo Crew lasted about three months, and after it was over, they decided to keep me on staff as a "shadow," which is like being a zoo intern for the summer. You get to choose the department you want to work in and I picked the commissary because it handles all the animal food for the zoo. I had a vision of myself all dressed in khaki hopping on a golf cart, driving up to an exhibit, and hand-feeding a bundle of fresh vegetables to an adorable animal. But that's not what people at the commissary actually do—they don't feed the animals, they just make the food and then the zookeeper takes it to the animals. This was disappointing, to say the least.

In the commissary I ended up spending all day making food in a huge industrial zoo kitchen, often all alone. I had two bosses, Jim and Barry, but they were both pretty weird. Plus, I think they felt uncomfortable because they were both guys in their forties and they had this scrawny fifteen-year-old girl following them around. So they were pretty hands-off.

The kitchen was one big room covered with giant

whiteboards on all sides. On the whiteboards were recipes for all the different animals' meals. I would just start at one end and work my way around. I'd always start with the fruit salad for the parrots. After the parrots I'd move on to the elephants and make their salad. This is how I learned about different lettuce varieties, like romaine and red leaf lettuce. I'd layer them all together and make sure the carrots were cut properly and toss together a giant salad in a bucket.

I would be standing at the counter chopping for hours with these huge knives I had never used before. A lot of the fruit dishes I made had to be put through this giant industrial chopper. When I think back on that machine, I could have easily cut my hand off. But I was so timid and shy that I just did what Barry said and put the fruit in there. Most of the time I was in that room by myself with a stupid transistor radio crackling and playing awful country music. I was too nervous to ask, "Hey, could I change the channel?"

Then there was the freezer. It was huge and dark and filled with bags of baby mice, big mice, rats, guinea pigs, and all the things the snakes want to eat. Some snakes were tiny, and I had to know "Okay, they get six baby mice," and I'd go in and get six tiny, pink, frozen baby mice that weren't even bigger than a peanut. For the pythons I'd have to pull out whole guinea pigs with frozen tails and everything. At first this was really intense for me because it was just a lot of dead animals, but eventually I got used to it and tried to think of the dead, frozen mice as something more like frozen shrimp you'd buy at the grocery store.

The freezer was bad, but not the worst. The worst was the day Barry brought a huge bucket into the kitchen. He was smiling about it—you could tell he thought this was going to be really funny. He put the bucket in the sink and took the cover off. It was filled with dark red cows' blood. We're talking a ten-gallon bucket of blood. And Barry just said, "Okay, this is for the vampire bats." He reached down in there and pulled up this giant blob and threw it into the sink. And he looked at me and said, "You need to find all these chunks of coagulated blood and pull them out so we can divide them into containers." I was horrified. But my shyness prevented me from asking any questions, so I just . . . did it. What else was there to do? I have this really vivid memory of reaching into a giant bucket of cows' blood and pulling out these huge clots while this transistor radio is playing Garth Brooks in the background. I did that for an entire day, just pulled chunks out of a blood bucket. At the end of the day I got in my mom's car, we picked up some Taco Bell, and everything was normal.

After a while Jim and Barry stopped being in that room with me at all. They just let me do anything. I started to jazz up the recipes a bit. I took a lot of liberties with the parrot fruit salad. On Monday I could say, "Let's do apple and pineapple" and on Tuesday I would serve kiwi and mango. I liked that kind of responsibility; I found it very motivating.

I did finally get a chance to feed an animal that summer: I took a giant pinecone covered in peanut butter and chocolate chips to a cute little Asian black bear named Maria. I went inside her cage to give her the pinecone and, I swear, she put her arm around me. That made it all worth it.

—HANNAH HAYES, *twenty-seven, is a food editor at* Southern Living *in Birmingham, Alabama, where she works in a very different kind of professional kitchen.*

The Tormented Sandwich Assistant

1988

In high school my friends and I used to hang out at this one deli all the time. I'll call it Frank's. It was a small place between a dry cleaner and a judo studio that only had about eight tables, but they baked their own bread and made these *incredible* sandwiches. I grew up in a kosher home so I always ordered a veggie sandwich that had a whole sliced-up avocado with cheese and really nice tomato, crunchy lettuce, and a homemade mayo spread. It was served on a hot, crispy baguette that was just so, so good.

The best part was the owner, Frank, who was really nice to us. He was a wiry guy, probably in his fifties, with a big shock of white hair and an exotic accent. He was always super friendly. When we walked in, he'd say, "Come in, sit down.

What are you eating today?" That kind of thing. As teenagers we weren't really used to being treated that way so we'd leave, saying to ourselves, "Frank is so awesome, he's so cool, he's just like one of us."

One day we walked in and there was a Help Wanted sign up. I had never really had a job but I did have an interest in restaurants and cooking, so I asked if he would hire me and he said, "Sure!" I was kind of surprised how easy it was, but I was scheduled to start the next week, just working a few days after school.

Almost immediately I realized that Frank was a complete asshole. Like, from the minute I got behind the counter he was yelling at me. He criticized every single thing that I did. I couldn't even separate the presliced pieces of cheese correctly for this guy. I was supposed to use this huge slicer to cut the meat and he had this way of doing it where his hands would get insanely close to the blade. I wasn't comfortable doing it that way and he would yell and call me a wimp. Oh, and the avocados, that was a huge sore spot. I could not cut an avocado that met this guy's standards! It was hilarious because I ate so many of those avocados as a customer, but he swore I wasn't slicing them right.

The first day was the worst because I was so shocked at the one-hundred-eighty-degree personality flip. I mean, I was just confused more than anything. I remember thinking that I wanted to quit on the first day, but I thought to myself, "No, you're not a quitter, you can't quit." I thought I could charm him or just outlast him and he'd eventually calm down. But he never did. And he was not interested in teaching me anything, so I stopped even hoping that I could get better.

When I told my friends they genuinely did not believe me; they thought it was impossible that he could be like that. This was the nice guy we had been seeing at the deli for years, and now he was screaming at me and telling me that I'd never be able to make a proper sandwich in my entire life?

One day, about three weeks in, he wanted me to cook up some bacon. The truth was, I didn't know how to cook bacon because I grew up in a kosher home. So I nervously said, "Um, I don't really know how . . ." and he just got this look of horror on his face. He looked truly appalled. And then he fired me. I believe his exact words were "This is not going to work out." It was shocking, obviously, because I'd never been fired before and, even though I hated the job, I was actually kind of crushed. It was a huge blow.

After he canned me, my friends completely stopped going there, and I certainly never went in there again. My family's dry cleaner was next door so I used to have to drive there and park in front occasionally and I was always scared that I would have to see him and make eye contact or something. A few years later I drove by and noticed that Frank's had closed and I can't say that I was really all that sad about it. But still, those were some damn good sandwiches.

—ADEENA SUSSMAN *graduated from culinary school and is a recipe developer, cookbook author, and food writer. She's been working in the food world for fifteen years and can now slice an avocado like a pro.*

The Slacking Scooper

2000

I was a cheerleader in high school. Not the kind of cheerleader who carries pom-poms at football games, but the really intense kind. The kind you see on ESPN. I mean, you had to know how to do a standing tuck just to make the squad.

We competed in the big National Cheerleading Association competition every year, and we'd always rank in the top ten in the country. Our coach was serious. I lived in a suburb outside of Salt Lake City, right near some of the best skiing in the world, and we weren't even allowed to go on the mountain because she was afraid we would tear an ACL or break a leg. We practiced almost twenty hours a week. Needless to say, all of my friends were also cheerleaders.

One day one of the girls on the cheer squad came to practice with some really good news: There was an ice cream shop opening in my town that was supposed to be just like Cold

Stone Creamery, where you get toppings mixed right into your ice cream. We all loved Cold Stone, but the nearest one was fifteen minutes away, so this was a big deal to us. She got a job there, and said we all should apply.

We basically did everything together already, so this made a lot of sense to me. I didn't need the money, I just did it because all my friends were doing it, and we thought it would be fun. It was a very high school mentality—one person had the idea and we all jumped on the bandwagon. So literally six of us cheerleaders went over to apply; I don't know what the owner was thinking, but he hired us all right away.

The first day I wore platform flip-flops, which was one clue that I was vastly underprepared for what went on behind the ice cream counter. We'd have to dip the ice cream scoops in hot water, which made the ice cream easier to scoop, but the milky water would fly all over the floor, so the floor got really slippery. Flip-flops were pretty much the worst idea ever, not to mention disgusting. I had watery milk in between my toes and I was sliding all over the place that first day. It was way more dangerous than skiing!

As it turns out, us cheerleaders weren't the only ones who were excited about the new ice cream shop. At night, it felt like the whole town came in. There would be lines out the door! I probably knew about 50 percent of the customers who walked in, which meant that 50 percent of the time I was hiding because I hated seeing people I knew. I was embarrassed to be working in a service job and I knew I looked hideous in my purple T-shirt uniform. My arm would start to hurt from scooping so much ice cream halfway through my shift, but the people just kept lining up; it was never-ending. I never learned how to make the milkshakes; instead I developed a different skill: inventing excuses to pawn those orders off onto other workers.

The tipping point was right after I got my driver's license. My dad said he would buy me a car, and we had gone to pick it out together. I was so excited. I was at work when he went to pick it up from the dealership, and he drove by the ice cream shop, honking and waving at me from my car! I was just like, "What am I doing?? I don't have to work! I could be at home sitting by the pool and driving my new car, but instead I'm scooping ice cream."

I wanted to quit so badly, and soon I had the perfect excuse: One of the cheerleaders' wrist started hurting, so she went to the doctor who told her she might have carpal tunnel syndrome from scooping ice cream. She was really, really scared. If it got worse she'd have to stop tumbling and then she wouldn't be able to compete. She might even have to leave the cheer squad.

When she told us, we all immediately freaked out—we were worried about carpal tunnel ruining our own cheer careers, of course! So, the most responsible girl in our squad—the one who eventually became cheer captain—called the owner and said, "We're running the risk of carpal tunnel syndrome, so we're all quitting right now." The owner was really pissed, and we knew we could never show our faces in there again.

The next summer I got a job at Nordstrom, where I worked throughout high school and college until I moved to New

York. I loved working there. I met my husband there! It was a world away from the ice cream shop because it was related to what I ultimately wanted to do: It made me realize I wanted to be in the fashion industry. Plus, it didn't make me smell like milk.

—ALI PEW, *thirty, is now a fashion editor at* InStyle *magazine in New York City. She never developed carpal tunnel syndrome.*

WHEN LIFE HANDS YOU LESSONS

The Things We Learned the Hard Way

The Flower Wholesaler

1985

When I was eight years old my family went on a vacation to Hawaii, where we saw protea flowers for the first time. They are really striking flowers that kind of look like colorful pincushions. We had never seen anything like them before, but they were on all the tables at our hotel and we thought they were just the craziest flowers we'd ever seen. My parents are curious people, so they were asking everyone at the hotel where the flowers came from. When they finally tracked down the source, we went to the florist where the protea came from. We saw a field with protea growing everywhere. My parents could not stop taking pictures.

When my parents got home they found a little shop in San Diego that had started importing these flowers. We planted them in our backyard in Santa Ana and they started to grow like crazy! Suddenly we had all these different kinds of protea plants and they were going nuts.

Like us, most of the people in our neighborhood had never seen protea before, and they were intrigued. My parents had some friends who owned a flower shop and when they came over one day and saw all the flowers, they suggested that we sell them to their shop. That was how it started.

At first we were only selling to the one shop, but I was a very outgoing eight-year-old. I wore neon shorts and animal-print button downs and bright socks . . . I definitely had my own thing going on, and it was bold. I had no problem striking up conversations with strangers, so my mom drove my older brother and me to florists around town to talk to them about buying our flowers. She'd stay in the car and we'd just walk in and show them our protea. They'd get really excited because they'd never seen them before. We really had a monopoly on this market. We were selling these flowers for like $1.25 each and the bigger ones, the king protea, we would sell for four dollars. That's a lot when you're eight years old! We were just killing it.

My brother, who was twelve, declared himself the businessman and the bookkeeper. He came up with a whole accounts receivable system where we would give the flowers to the florists and, as the flowers sold, the florist would pay us. It seemed pretty complicated to keep track of all this, but I didn't really understand what was going on. I was mainly in charge of cutting flowers for our orders and taking care of the protea and spraying the plants with Raid when they got infested with ants, which was often.

My brother later admitted that he had no idea what he was doing and that there were no "books" in his bookkeeping job—he'd just scribble on the back of old printer paper. He was like a little Bernie Madoff, just making shit up, but it seemed like he was really busy and we were doing well, so things went on like this for a while.

Eventually, after about a year of protea prosperity, more professional florists began to import protea themselves and we experienced competition for the first time. Our prices were driven down. I'll never forget the feeling of going into a florist and seeing that they already had protea flowers, but they weren't ours. It was rough.

A few florists stayed loyal. I remember one of our customers told us that she would always buy our protea because they smelled so nice. But the thing is, protea don't really have a fragrance. What she was smelling was the scented Raid I was using to keep the ants away.

As the competition increased, things between me and my brother started to get tense. Basically, I wised up and realized that I was doing all the work. I was down there spraying and cutting the flowers and getting all of our deliveries ready while my brother was just sitting there. So I started a one-man labor strike. I told him he had to do half the work to get half the money, and he said, "Okay, fine, let's just not do this anymore." So that was the end of the business.

It was a good lesson in collaboration. I think partnerships are really hard. I've seen that in a lot of instances in my career. I see all these people starting clothing lines together, and it's always easy in the beginning. But when money gets involved it can be so tough. I experienced that even at a very early age.

But I also think that it's important to not be afraid to try and fail at different things. You should always be looking for a great opportunity. If something comes up and it looks different from what you're doing, try it! Take every chance. Those proteas that just happened to be growing in my yard were an opportunity that we saw. When you see it, go for it. If it doesn't work out forever, that's fine.

—TODD SELBY, *thirty-seven, is a photographer, director, author, and illustrator. He has published three books,* The Selby in Your Place, Edible Selby, *and* Fashionable Selby, *which highlight the personal spaces, work, and fashion of creative individuals. See his work at theselby.com.*

The Tech Go-Getter

2001

Growing up, I always had this general philosophy that, basically, went like this: If something was really hard, that was the thing I should try to do. So when I was a freshman at Rice University and a guy I knew got a really coveted internship at Microsoft, that internship became my new goal.

I had no idea what I really wanted to do in life, but I knew that an internship at Microsoft was hard to get, so that meant it pretty much fulfilled all my requirements. At that point Google was just a new, tiny search engine, and a job at Microsoft was *the* job. Microsoft was the monstrosity. People hated Microsoft because they were so successful. I was instantly starry-eyed.

Sophomore year I signed up for an in-person interview with the Microsoft intern recruiters. I borrowed a car and drove it to downtown Houston for the interview. I walked into the Hilton looking for the conference room where the interview was supposed to take place, only to learn that it was actually scheduled for the Hyatt, not the Hilton. By then it was too late—I had missed the interview.

I pleaded with the recruiter to interview me anyway, and he gave in. He came to my dorm room and we did the interview there. I thought it went pretty well. But four weeks later I got a little postcard telling me I was rejected. So, there goes my summer job.

The following year I redoubled my efforts. This time, I practiced for months for that interview. I wasn't a computer science major, but I read an entire computer science algorithms book because I knew they might be asking about that. Back then brainteasers were a popular thing at Microsoft, so I memorized every brainteaser I could find on the Internet. I wrote paragraphs and paragraphs of responses to hypothetical interview questions. I did mock interviews with myself in the car, just talking to myself the whole way.

When I went home for Christmas I took the family camera into my sister's bedroom, set it up on a tripod and videotaped myself answering the interview questions they had asked me the year before. This was a very awkward thing to do, to sit in a room by myself and talk to a camera, but watching it was even weirder. I was mainly looking for how I presented myself. Did I look confident in what I was saying? Did I use my hands in an appropriate manner?

By the time I was going back for the interview, I didn't question myself at all. I was dressed in a full suit and I knew everything inside out. I blew through the first interview, no problem. Then they flew me to Seattle for an interview on the Microsoft campus and took me out to a nice steak dinner. It was a very big deal.

I got the internship. I spent a whole summer in Seattle and it was amazing. I had money for the first time and a big group of tech friends. No one was the cool kid on campus, so we all nerded out together. I turned twenty-one and we partied hard.

We were each paid $4,600 a month for the summer, which is a lot of money when you're twenty-one. I saved a ton of that money and thought about all the things I was going to use it for when I got home. But, as soon as I was back, my dad made me write a check to my college for tuition, and all of it was gone in a single check. It is still, today, the largest check I have ever cut. It put a very, very real reckoning as to how much my education was costing. I mean, I worked all summer for that and it only paid for *one* semester. I never skipped a class again.

During my internship, I learned that the most difficult group to get a job with in Microsoft was the Windows security group. At the time, security was really hot in the tech scene. It wasn't particularly sexy; it was anti-spam, anti-virus, secure passwords, that kind of stuff. I knew nothing about this. Zero. But it was the hard thing to get, so I decided it should be my new goal.

The next semester I basically snuck into a graduate-level security class, learned enough to be confident, and, miraculously, passed the class. So that year I went back to interview at Microsoft, this time for a full-time job with the security team, and I got it. At this point I was pretty happy with myself because it was November and I already had a job, the kind of job every graduate wanted.

The rest of my year was pretty fun. I never really drank that much, but after I got that job, all bets were off. I started *really* having fun. I even told Microsoft I wanted to push back my start date so I could take some time to travel. I went to Brazil, learned Portuguese, went to India . . . it was great, and it was all because I had this amazing thing lined up. Finally, I showed up at Microsoft ready for real life to begin. I found an apartment, and I got to work.

It turns out, I really hated the job. I mean, I *really* hated it. And there was no hope: I didn't want to be my boss; I didn't want to be my manager. It was only a few months in when it dawned on me: I had spent years to get here, but I didn't really ever *decide* this. I just kept chasing the next hard thing, the next accomplishment. For years I had always just worked on tackling what was next and moving up. And all of a sudden, the "next thing" seemed kind of crappy.

It took about two years before I got up the courage to leave Microsoft, but when I did I left cold turkey. No plans. I knew I had to find something to do, but I knew this was not it. I went to Brazil, I came back, and everyone kept asking me, "What are you going to do?" The only thing I could say was "I have no idea." I was on my own in Seattle for four years after I left Microsoft. I was just rubbing two sticks together trying to make something work before I figured out that, if I wanted to be in tech, I should move to San Francisco and do it my way.

I learned a tough lesson during my time at Microsoft: Just because you *can* do something, doesn't mean you should. Up until I was twenty-five I only wanted what other people wanted. I tried to get into elite schools and picked the most prestigious major. That was how I thought about things, which was a mistake. A departure from that mentality was a huge shift for me personally. I finally realized that the best thing to do is to make proactive decisions about what you want in life—not what everyone else wants—and find the job that gets you there.

—CRAIG DOS SANTOS, *thirty-three, is an entrepreneur in San Francisco who founded and sold a mobile app start-up. He now coaches other entrepreneurs in nego-tiation skills and blogs about it at craigdossantos.com.*

The Very Late Bloomer

1990

It's funny, I've grown up to be a very, very hardworking adult, but that wasn't always the case. My parents must have been very indulgent because they never pushed me to work, ever. When I graduated from college I was profiled by the *Brown Daily Herald*. They wrote about two different seniors, one of whom was super motivated and had his shit together and had a job on Wall Street. That was not me. I was profiled as "the clueless senior" who had no idea what he was going to do and had no prospects. I was quoted as saying something like, "I don't know what I'm going to do; I'm probably going to move to Santa Fe and become a basket weaver."

I delayed my entry into the workplace a year by taking pottery classes at the Rhode Island School of Design, or RISD, after college. During that year I made a couple of aborted attempts to get a job. I tended bar for one night. Somebody roped me into this thing where, for twenty-five bucks, I would go to banks and be a kind of secret shopper to judge their level of cleanliness and friendliness. I spent two hours at orientation and then I did one bank job and never went back. So that was the entirety of my work experience: about three hours in my life. That makes me sound terribly spoiled, which I suppose I was.

So, needless to say, I wasn't awfully prepared when I decided to move to New York City. It was 1989 and the economy was a disaster. When I arrived there was a phone strike in progress, so not only was there no Internet because it wasn't invented yet, but there was no phone. For the first three months I was here I sort of tried to find a job without the Internet or the phone or any work experience. It wasn't going well.

So there I was, twenty-two, completely inexperienced and naive. No plan, nothing. I was anxious and thinking, "Well, I was a good student but I guess I'm going to be a failed adult." Then a friend of mine said to me, "You like TV, you should be a talent agent." I was highly suggestible, having no ambition or plan or skill of my own, so I thought, "Okay!" That suddenly became my focus and I began blindly sending out résumés.

On my résumé, which was very, very short, I had a section called "skills and interests." My interests, I believe, included "squash" and in the skills section I had written "faxing." I don't know how I picked up that skill but it turned out to be incredibly important.

One day I got a call from a guy named Julio who ran the

mailroom at a small, up-and-coming talent agency. I thought, "Okay, working in the mailroom is a narrative I'm familiar with, that's a real thing." So I went in for an interview.

I wore a jacket and tie that I borrowed from a friend. I got there and quickly realized that Julio didn't know Brown from RISD and he didn't care. But he said, "Wow, so where have you faxed?" I think I faked it and said, "Oh, I fax all the time." And he said, "Really?" And I said, "Oh yeah, you know, you just unfurl the thingy and you have to load the paper the right way—it's gotta be the right side up!" And he was like, "Okay, great, because this job involves a lot of fax-ing." I nailed the interview with Julio and I got the job.

Julio proved to be prophetic because the job did involve a lot of faxing, and a lot of photocopying as well. Photocopy-ing scripts and manuscripts, that sort of thing. It was very menial, which was fine. I learned a lot about what adulthood is, which is menial. That's sort of the nature of the beast, what-ever your job is, it tends to be task-oriented.

I had been doing that for a couple of months when a gay agent, who will remain nameless, spotted me and fancied me in a very sweet sort of way and hired me to be his assistant. I was not an Adonis or anything but I was young and cute enough and I guess that was all it took. The not-so-sweet part was that his actual assistant at the time was a very serious, motivated person, and he got demoted back to the mailroom. Isn't that awful?

So my faxing and my masculine wiles are what got me into that chair. My first promotion! This was before comput-ers were in every office so my responsibilities included typing

up my boss's to-do list every day on my typewriter. Then I'd
make a list of the calls that he had to make, and then just sort
of dealt with whatever came up. I was "on" all day, scheduling appointments for actors to go meet casting agents. Which,
to be perfectly honest, I had about zero interest in. Now that
I think about it, I could not possibly have cared less about an
actor meeting a casting agent. I was not starstruck at all.

I became very chummy with the other assistants. We'd
all gather around the watercooler in the morning and chit-
chat. It was like being in a typing pool in the fifties except
we were all gay, modern guys. We would talk about which
clients were cute, who was doing what in the office, what
everyone was wearing, that kind of thing.

I also grew increasingly friendly with my boss. We would
go away for weekends to clients' houses. Then we would start
to have these long lunches together, go shopping together, that
sort of thing. We got really close and became the talk of the
office. Cut to: We're dating. So I'm answering his phone by
day and dating him by night. It was complicated.

I knew everyone was gossiping about us, but I remained
really friendly with the other assistants. I remained especially
friendly with one assistant in particular. And then I started
having an affair with him. So there I am, sleeping with my
boss and my colleague. It was so ridiculous. That probably
lasted for about a month and then my boss found out. I still
don't know how, but he did. He called me into the office and
said, "You've got to leave the company." Of course he was
right.

I remember at the time a friend of mine was like, "What

are you going to do, are you going to sue?" and I was like, "Sue? I'm cheating on him! Why would I sue?" Instead I asked my boss if he would help me get another job and he said, "Fine." So there was one very tense month when he had already fired me but I was still there, waiting for another offer.

Eventually I got a job working at another talent agency and then I got fired from that. And then I got fired from the next job. This pattern continued for about three years.

Before I had that first job, being unemployed felt a little more carefree, but after that first job it was more pathos-drenched because I felt like I had failed. I had slept my way to the bottom. The thing is, it turned out fine. During the time that I was "looking for a job," at age twenty-six, I started what would grow to be my own company, something I never could have imagined for myself.

The main thing I tell young people about work is just to chill the fuck out. I really think you shouldn't even be remotely introspective about your station in life until you're thirty. I really, sincerely believe that. People are way too careerist. Chill a bit. Now I have built a really strange, idiosyncratic business and it's really a function of the fact that I was not careerist. I think there's something to be said about meandering a bit.

—JONATHAN ADLER, *forty-eight, is a potter and designer with more than twenty-five eponymous boutiques worldwide. He is happily married to Simon Doonan, Creative Ambassador of Barneys, whom he did not meet in the office.*

The Ice Cream Shop Education

1984

My mother told me I had to get a job because I refused to do any after-school activities and she wasn't going to let me lie around the house. She drove me to the strip mall and our first stop was McDonald's. I walked in, this tall, clean-cut all-American girl with blond hair and blue eyes, and I went up to the counter to ask for an application. The manager immediately came out and sat down with me and, after a few minutes, said, "Okay, yeah fine, you can get a job here." I don't think I had even finished the application.

Working at McDonald's stunk. It was the quintessential all-American first job, but it was really awful. The uniforms were maroon and yellow polyester—so uncomfortable. All the tasks were my least favorite tasks. Working the fryer, cooking the burgers, doing the cash register . . . they were all awful. But it was a job.

The manager of the Baskin-Robbins next door would come in for lunch every day, so I got to know who he was and I realized that, because I made minimum wage at McDonald's, there was really nowhere to go but up, and at least the ice cream place wouldn't smell like grease, right? So the next time he came in I asked him, "Are you hiring?" and he said, "Yeah, you know, we could probably use someone else." So I promptly quit McDonald's and went to work next door.

I liked the job. Scooping ice cream was great, with the exception of the Popeye forearms I would get during the summer. We could choose the radio station, it was a lot more relaxed than McDonald's, and I had a lot of colleagues my own age. It was exactly the kind of job you'd want to have as a teenager.

After about six months of working there I decided I wanted a raise. I needed more money to buy records, because that was really all I cared about at the time. So I asked the boss and he told me he would give me fifty cents more per hour if I would decorate the cakes, and I said okay. His wife trained me; she had been coming in to decorate the cakes and now she got to stay home with her kids. Fifty cents extra an hour didn't sound like a lot but I calculated that it would add up to about a thousand more dollars a year. That was a lot of money!

Learning how to ask for that first raise was a great experience. It was a lesson that has paid off for me tremendously in my career. I still don't like negotiating, but I learned that if I come into negotiations with a good justification or a trade-off I can propose, it will *always* work. It has helped me in a number of different jobs I have had. Now I am middle aged and I've been a working professional for decades and I still remember that first raise.

Everything was going well in my new position as ice cream scooper slash cake decorator until one night when I was closing the shop. It was empty, I was bored, and there was nothing happening. I had gotten everything done and as soon as I was out of there I'd get to go home. A lady came by and knocked on the door and I said, "Oh sorry, we're closed," and she said, "But it's not time yet!" That was true, we were still a few minutes away from closing time, but I shrugged and said, "Well, we're closed," and she left.

The next day the manager called me and said, "I need to talk to you." When I came in he said, "Someone called me yesterday and said that you closed early last night." And I said, "Yeah, I did." He said, "I can't let you get away with that, you're going to have to quit." I felt bad but also incredibly stupid. It would have been so easy for me to open that door and just let her in and serve her the single scoop of ice cream she probably wanted.

It's one of those things you do as a kid that you think, "Well, what could it matter?" but clearly it matters to someone. I think about it now when I have to deal with disciplining or changing someone's behavior at work. Sometimes people do stupid things and it's usually because they don't think about the effect it could have on someone else. I think that was one of the lessons I learned: Someone is paying you to do a job, to help their business, so just do it. No shortcuts. But I'm sure that he, as a manager, also learned that if you leave a sixteen-year-old in charge of things, they're going to do the kind of things that sixteen-year-olds do.

—SAMANTHA WESTCOTT, *forty-six, is a manager at Children's Hospital Los Angeles, where she has been on the other side of the table for negotiations about raises and tough discussions of firings.*

The Fishy Situation

1965

I went to the University of Illinois on a full football scholarship as an offensive guard. It wasn't like it is now, where there's tons of supervision for the players and summers are spent working out. The football program would actually get us summer jobs that let us earn some money. They would arrange with different businesses to hire us athletes for the summer and they made sure those jobs paid well.

That's how I ended up with a job at a fish company in Chicago. I was a delivery driver, which paid good money, probably five bucks an hour, which was about double the minimum wage. My boss was Mr. Gambini, the owner of the fish company. He seemed to like me. We both had Italian last names, so we got along pretty good.

On my first day, he asked me if I could drive, and when I said I could, he gave me a small Toyota pickup truck and a few deliveries to make on the northwest side of Chicago. The truck was filled with crates of fish and seafood that had ice all over the top.

I was headed to one of the nicest restaurants in Chicago to deliver their daily fish order. I was driving along with the radio blaring and came up to a stop sign. I stopped, looked both ways, and started to go through the intersection when all of a sudden another car came speeding through and slammed into the side of my truck. The whole car flipped over on its side and cases of fish flew everywhere. I had to stand up and reach above my head to climb out of the door.

This was pre–cell phone days, of course, so I went to find a pay phone. Someone had already called the police, so my first call was to Mr. Gambini. I said, "Mr. Gambini, I've had an automobile accident." He said, "Are you okay?" And I said, "Mr. Gambini, I have to tell you, they are stealing the fish." He said, "What are you talking about, they're stealing the fish?" I said, "The fish are all over the ground and the kids are just taking it!" We had lobster and red snapper and all this really nice, fresh fish. People were just picking it up and walking off with it, I had no idea what to do. He said, "Don't worry about the fish!"

The police came and they gave me the ticket because they claimed that the other driver had the right of way and that I had gone too soon. I didn't agree with that. I went back to the fish company and told Mr. Gambini about the ticket and he said, "Let my lawyer help you take care of that." So I agreed. The next day, I went to work and Mr. Gambini gave me a bigger truck. He said, "See if you can roll this one."

My court date was about a month later. I went down to the court to visit with the lawyer before we had to appear before the judge. I was so nervous. I asked the lawyer, "What should I say? Should I explain to the judge what happened?" and the lawyer said, "No, just keep your mouth shut." We went into the courtroom and waited for my case to be called. Finally, the judge hit the gavel and it started.

"Is the defendant Mr. Carbonari here?" the judge asked. My lawyer stood up and said, "Yes, the defendant is here," and then the judge said, "Is the officer here?" and there was nothing. He asked again. Nothing. I think he said it three times and then he said, "Case dismissed."

We started to walk out of the courtroom and I was thanking the lawyer for his help when I see the officer sitting out in the hallway, just waiting for my case to be over. It turns out that the officer was paid off by my lawyer to skip the trial so that I would automatically win.

That was my introduction to this way of "taking care" of things, but it was Chicago in the 1960s, so it was not my last. My dad explained to me what had happened, because those things were just known then. He also taught me how to bribe police, just in case. He said that, if you were pulled over, you could ask a cop, "Can't we talk about this over lunch?" That was the line that let him know you were willing to pay. And if the policeman was willing to receive, he'd say, "Sure," and you would give him the bills or he'd direct you to some nearby spot to leave cash. That went on a lot in those days. It was as much a part of Chicago government as a dead voter.

I worked at the fish company for the rest of the summer

and I'd commute back and forth on the bus. One day I'm sitting on the bus going home, and two young girls get on. Now, I'm sitting in the back with the windows open because I know I smell like fish a little bit. But these two girls are sitting there and they're saying, "I think it smells like fish . . ." And the other girl says, "Yeah, I smell that too! Like dead fish, I think it's *dead* fish." And they started looking around; they're looking under all the chairs for some dead fish. I'm sitting there, dying, just hoping they don't get too close. I made it off the bus just before they would have figured out it was me.

I had earned about $1,200 when I went back to school and that was enough to get me through the year. The biggest lesson I learned was that I didn't want to do that for a living! The other lesson was that you had to work harder at a small business. Yes, I would make deliveries, but there were only about seven employees, so sometimes I would have to work in the ice locker or clean up after the butchers. You kind of learn that your job is never just one single thing, it's a multitude of assignments. In my later life, when I owned my own business, that was a real critical thing. When you own a business you do whatever it takes to get it done. Though I can't say I ever paid off the cops for anyone.

—JERRY CARBONARI, *sixty-nine, started his own business, which grew to twenty-one employees. He sold the company and is now retired.*

The Growing Gardener

2013

I got my first job last year, when I was sixteen, and I've learned so much since then. My job was as a farmer at the Supa Fresh Youth Farm, but it was really a lot more than farming. "Cultivating the future," that's the mission statement.

Before I started at the farm they put everyone through a two-week training class about working and getting a job. We learned how to apply for a job and how to interview. The bosses even gave us mock interviews and helped us learn how to answer certain questions. They taught us to walk in nice and tall and even practice our handshake to make sure it's strong and firm but not to the point where you'd crush someone's hand. It's all about the first impression, you know?

They recommended we wear skirts or slacks for the interview and they set up accounts for us at a store to go buy interview clothes. I picked out slacks with a white shirt and a blazer, just something really simple and nice. When I put on that outfit in the dressing room I tried to imagine myself as the interviewer. I looked at myself in the mirror and saw myself walking into the interview room. I saw that I looked really professional. The training period was about more than working on the farm, it was preparing you for the real world.

When it came time to start on the farm, we just dove right in. It was actually really rough at first because it was a very hot summer and we were out there all day. There were so many different jobs to do and I wanted to do all of them. There was watering, harvesting, and weeding . . . a lot of weeding.

I was really, really worried when I first started because I am handicapped. I have a condition that is hard to explain but it means that I don't have total control over my left leg. So I can feel everything but I can't move it. I have crutches to get around, which makes it really hard to bend down or squat and so I was worried that I wouldn't be able to do much, or that I wouldn't be able to do the job at all. But the bosses, they got me a little movable bench that had a cushion and wheels so I could just sit down and wheel to the side of my weeding area. And it had a little storage place where I could keep my tools. They made it real easy for me, and I couldn't stop thanking them for that. They made me feel like I could do something really good for that place. Even the other teen-agers helped me—they were so awesome. Everyone thought I could do it and that made me think I could do it too.

Pretty soon our garden was just producing and produc-ing. We sell our produce at a farmer's market and we do a CSA [Community Supported Agriculture] share and they were always just stocked to the brim with so many veggies. I got to go work at the farmer's market, which helped me practice my customer service skills. I felt amazing every time someone bought something. I like to tell the customers that we've seen all of these veggies grow from tiny little seeds and become big beets or carrots. It's so awesome to see it all grow into what we're selling and to imagine people using them in their dinner.

People also liked to know whether it was grown organically. We're not certified organic because it takes quite a bit of time and money to get certified. So we tell them about how we practice organic methods and we don't use any pesticides or herbicides or any of that. Everything is weeded and watered by hand. It's all us, nothing else. I felt like a real salesperson, because I sold quite a bit of that produce!

My friends who work at other places tell me that when they got their first jobs they were kind of expected to fail. Not completely fail, but they didn't have high standards set for them. They weren't expected to accomplish much and everyone thought they would be slackers. But on the Supa farm they know what teenagers are like. They have a lot of trust and belief in us and I think that makes us all feel good.

Ever since that job I have wanted my own little garden or bed, so this summer I rented a bed at a community garden for me and my family. They actually gave me one for free; it was so nice. It's mostly food, but there are some flowers because, I'm not gonna lie, I love flowers too. There are tons of tomatoes, which are producing so much; every week I come back and there's more. They're really delicious cherry tomatoes; the only problem is that while I'm standing out there picking them I can't stop eating them! By the time I finish there is just half of what I picked in the basket.

This summer I went back to the farm to work for a second year. My parents think it's awesome that I am working and learning. It's nice that I get money out of it but, honestly, I am just working to learn how to farm and to meet new people.

I never thought I'd get so much from a job. I didn't know what kind of work I could do because of my handicap but it turned out fine. It turned out better than fine—way better than I ever imagined. I never thought I'd be able to do all these things and I've never felt as much confidence in myself. That helps me in school too, like with speeches and presentations. I used to be so shy but now I'm one of the first to volunteer to give a presentation—I mean, not completely first, second or third is fine with me—but I don't second-guess myself as much as I did before that summer.

I feel so blessed because not many people, teens, get this chance to do a job like this with bosses that are so great and know what it's like. My mom always told me that I should be thankful that I found something like this and I'm like, "Yes, I am crazy thankful."

—TYRA TANAKA, *seventeen, is about to graduate from high school. For more information on the Supa Fresh Farm in Tigard, Oregon, visit supafreshyouthfarm.org.*

The High-Society Seater

1961

I had just gotten my associate's degree in hotel management and, like pretty much everyone else with that degree, I wanted to be the general manager of a hotel someday. So I moved to New York City and started off as the low man on the totem pole: a seater at the restaurant in the St. Regis.

The restaurant was at the very top of the St. Regis hotel and it had a fancy dining room that could seat about two hundred people and, on most nights, had a live orchestra that people could dance to. All the society people of New York dined there.

A seater is an entry-level job in the industry and it's the lowest position in the formal dining room hierarchy. The person who runs the dining room is called the maître d'hôtel and under him are captains. The captains take the orders and hand them to a runner who gives the orders to the kitchen.

But before all this happens, people are shown to their seat by me, the seater. The maitre d' would assign the tables ahead of time at a chart on the front podium and the seater could look at the chart and lead people to their table.

During my interview the manager asked, "Have you ever done this before?" and I said, "No, but I've read about it and I know what to do." That was good enough for him. He introduced me to Rudy, the maître d'hôtel, who said, "Fine, be here at five o'clock on Thursday." I had the job.

Rudy was European and he could speak four or five languages. He had been in the industry about forty years and people would call him for advice on menu planning or what wine to drink. He was very experienced, and he could have been a pompous ass. I mean, he really could have, plenty of maîtres d'hôtel are! But he was incredibly nice to me. At the end of the night Rudy would always make sure I went home with twenty dollars in cash. If I had made twelve dollars in tips he would give me eight dollars out of his own pocket so that I had twenty.

Usually I would get there about five o'clock, wearing my tuxedo, and Rudy would tell me what was going on that evening. Then he would go eat dinner and I would answer the phones. One night when I came in he told me, "Bill, we're really busy tonight, don't take anyone else." And I said, "Okay, Rudy, enjoy your dinner."

The second phone call that came through is a man who asks, "Is Rudy there?" So he obviously knew Rudy, which should have been my first clue. I said, "Sorry, Rudy stepped away for a moment, may I help you?" And he said, "This is

David Rockefeller. My wife and I are having a cocktail down in the King Cole Bar," which is a bar in the St. Regis. "We'd love to have dinner upstairs tonight." And I said, "Well, sir, I'm very sorry but Rudy has informed me that I'm not to take any more reservations tonight." There was a brief silence and then Mr. Rockefeller said, "Well, do me a favor, when Rudy returns will you just tell him that I called and that I'm downstairs?"

I had immediately recognized that last name. I mean, Rockefeller Center, Rockefeller Plaza, almost everything on Fifth Avenue had a Rockefeller name attached to it. But I also thought I should follow Rudy's orders. When he finally came back to the podium I said, "Rudy, I think I really screwed up," and told him about the call. He said, "It's fine, just call Pete, the manager down at the King Cole bar, and tell him to let Mr. Rockefeller know we have a table for him whenever he comes up."

I didn't have to tell him to be there at 7:15 or be there at 7:30 or anything like that, a table was just going to be there for him whenever he showed up! I found out later that Mr. Rockefeller was on the board of directors of this hotel, so he was probably not used to being told there was no room at the inn.

There was a long hallway from where the elevator opened up on our floor to where our podium was, so when the Rockefellers came up I could see them walking down the hall and I was just standing there. As they approached, Rudy stepped away from the podium and greeted them and said, "I'm very glad you could join us tonight, so happy you could come see us." He was a real professional and smoothed the situation out right away.

While Rudy was talking to Mr. Rockefeller, Mrs. Rockefeller looked at me sweating bullets and said quietly, "Young man, we understand, you were just doing your job." So nice, you know? And then Rudy turned to me and said, "Bill, please show the Rockefellers to their table." So I walked them over and, as I seated them, Mr. Rockefeller slipped me a folded-up five-dollar bill. Now, an average tip for a seater would be one or two dollars, so this was big. Five dollars in 1961! That's a tip I'll never forget.

—BILL SHORTER, *seventy-four, was the general manager of the Alta Club in Salt Lake City for thirteen years. He retired in 2007.*

The Help

1966

Out of ten kids in my family, I am number nine. There is a Southern term for that called the knee baby. The youngest is the arm baby and the second youngest is the knee baby, the one that's always hanging around down at the mother's knees while she holds the littlest baby. It was a term that stayed with me throughout my teenage years.

I was thirteen when I got my first job. My aunt Fannie was a domestic for an older woman and she asked me to come do the gardening on Saturdays. I'm not sure why my aunt chose the "knee baby" for this job—we came from a huge family and she had lots of other options—but I think she sized me up and figured I was responsible and would represent our family well.

A domestic is like a housekeeper, someone who does the cleaning and the cooking for a family. It was pretty prevalent back then, and I came from a long line of women who were domestics. This was dramatized in a recent movie called *The Help*, which was pretty accurate. Domestics almost felt like part of the family because they would stay at one house for thirty or forty years. In some cases, the domestics spent more time with the children of a family than their own parents did. So even when race relations got tense in the South, domestics often wanted to protect the people they worked for, and vice versa.

The woman I was working for was named Miss Wimpee; she was probably eighty or so. Her daughter was Miss Bonnie; she was about fifty. My aunt had been with Miss Wimpee for so long that she had helped raise Miss Bonnie. Miss Bonnie wasn't always there, but when I would go to work and see her car was there I always thought, "Oh no, I really gotta work today."

Miss Bonnie was a regional Girl Scout leader and a real outdoorsy person. She was what we used to call an "old maid" because she was fifty and had never been married. It was a very macho society back then and everyone thought if a woman wasn't married and submitting to a man there must be something wrong with her. But Bonnie was as smart and tough as anyone I ever met, male or female. She taught me how to cut lawns, pull weeds, prune, and fertilize, and she taught me how to do all this the proper way.

This job was pretty exciting as a teenager because I was earning a dollar an hour and getting a check every week. They didn't pay me in cash, they paid me in a real check, which I'd never seen before. It was a big deal getting a check, and taking it down to the corner store to cash it for a five-dollar bill and three ones. I was rolling in dough at age thirteen!

When summer came around and school was out I could work during the week. My cousin Thelma was a domestic for another family, the Smith family, and I started working in their yard. I loved it. Mrs. Smith, the mother in that house, was just a fantastic lady who would pick me up in her car, so I didn't have to ride my bike, and make me breakfast and delicious lunches. That was where I had beef Stroganoff for the first time. She made it for lunch and I just had to stop and ask, "Wow, what is this?" because it was so delicious. Plus, they paid me $1.50 per hour, not just a dollar.

The Smiths were a family of lawyers and they were very intelligent. Their vocabulary was exceptional and I learned how to speak like a really educated person by talking up to their level. There were three sons, and the youngest one, who was just a couple of years older than me, clearly looked down on me. He knew I was "the help." There was a real smugness about him. When I'd be outside cleaning and working in the hot sun he'd be in his bedroom with the air-conditioning on, just looking out the window. It certainly made me speak some words to myself under my breath. But his mom was so nice, she more than made up for him.

The beauty of youth is ignorant bliss, so I was just happy to have a job and get the money, I didn't notice the status until I was older. When I look back I think, "Oh, I was the help," but back then it was a privilege to have a job, especially as a knee baby. You were looked at differently around the neighborhood because you weren't a little boy playing all the time; you had real responsibility.

My next job was working in a restaurant. That was out of the heat, there was air-conditioning, and you could eat all the time. In my mind, it didn't get better than that.

—RANDOLPH WALKER, *sixty-one, is a sales associate at a department store in San Francisco, where he has worked for twenty-seven years.*

The Produce Picker

1961

I grew up in a small town in Massachusetts. It was a farming town, the kind of place where people say that there are more cows than people and it might actually be true. It was also home to these two brothers whose family owned a big farm. They reputedly had a falling-out some years back and split up the family farm, so there were two different farms and two different farm stands, both operating under the same last name, right across the highway from each other. Some people say it was just to increase business by getting a farm stand on each side of the street, that there was no real "falling-out" at all, but nonetheless people had their preferences.

When I turned thirteen, my father drove me up to the farm of his choice and I walked right up and said, "Can I work here this summer?" and the farmer said, "Sure." So it was a pretty intense job interview.

This farm belonged to Farmer Kelly, one of the feuding farmer brothers. He was a big Irish guy, a stern taskmaster and a hard worker. As a young man he had contracted polio and lost the use of his right arm. When the doctors asked him how they should arrange his paralyzed fingers he said, "Make them into a hook so I can lift bushel baskets." They did, and that's how he used his hand, as a hook. He was a farmer for life. All the kids who showed up to pick strawberries came pretty early, but he'd meet us with shoes already muddy from a day of work. He was always rather gruff, even to his two kids, who worked with us on the farm.

The first task at hand was picking strawberries, which were one of the earliest crops on the farm to ripen. All of us kids would pile into the back of a pickup truck with our wooden strawberry boxes to be driven up to the fields. We got some on-the-job training from Farmer Kelly: He came over and pointed to a greenish white strawberry and said, "See these? These aren't ready, so don't pick 'em." That was the extent of it. Then we were told to get to work.

That first week I was pretty motivated, I was picking strawberries like crazy. We were paid a whopping ten cents per quart and that first week I was picking four or five quarts an hour. I could have done even better if I wasn't eating so many. After a week, the thrill was gone and I dropped to two or three quarts per hour, with a few breaks to throw overly ripe strawberries at my fellow pickers. By the third week I couldn't even look at a strawberry anymore. I was completely sick of them.

After the strawberry season was done, the farmer kept

me on for the summer and I moved up to an hourly wage of fifty cents. That was the big deal, to be getting paid by the hour instead of by the quart. I'd pick corn and tomatoes, or do some weeding. Sometimes I'd ride with Farmer Kelly on his tractor. He'd run the cultivator on the fields and I'd have to run in front of it, picking up rocks that would get in the way and throwing them off to the side.

This was a real New England farm, complete with rocky terrain and big hills. I remember riding with Farmer Kelly up to a field at the very top of a hill on a particularly nice summer day. It was in a beautiful spot, with views on three sides, and when we got up there he said, "This is as close as you can get to God, being up here. When I come up here I like to just do my job and think." It surprised me, you know, because here's a guy that I see out here just grunt-laboring every day and he looks at it as a spiritual experience.

The more time I spent working with Farmer Kelly, the more I realized he was quite a guy.

What surprised me was that he was also an intellectual. To make money during the winter he sold encyclopedias, and he must have just read them all because he knew something about everything. One day I mentioned I was reading the Classics Illustrated version of *Moby Dick*. He said that was nice but I should be reading the original book and that I was not giving Melville any respect by missing his actual words and the many smaller stories in the novel.

From that day on we talked about books all the time. I don't remember all the books we talked about, but it seemed that he had read every single one. I became a pretty avid reader myself—it certainly made life in small-town Massachusetts more exciting.

> —STEVEN CARTER, *sixty-five, went on to be an English lit major at Bowdoin College in Maine. He now sells antiques across the East Coast and can finally eat strawberries again.*

The Self-Taught Sea Urchin Trader

1992

I'm Cambodian but I spent most of my childhood going back and forth between Cambodia and Vietnam because of the war. There was never really one place where I stayed; my mom and I did a lot of moving around for the first eight years of my life.

My mother was a very educated woman. She was one of the few women in our country who had gone to college and she had a job teaching French. But after the war started, my father was taken as a prisoner of war in Vietnam and we lost everything. All she could do was sell aspirin on the street as we traveled around looking for a safe place to live.

By 1971 or 1972, when the war got crazy and broke out everywhere, we tried to escape to Thailand by way of boat, meaning a shady guy would say, "Give me twenty thousand dollars and we'll try to get you to Thailand." We did this twice and it was unsuccessful both times. She gave them all of her money and jewelry to get us on that boat but, looking back, I think it was all a scam. They made us crouch in a boat, literally, for days. Not a big boat, I'm talking a boat the size of a canoe. We sat there, too scared to move, without food or water for four days. We never knew where we were because we were covered with a tarp, and then we'd pull up to shore and they'd say, "Sorry, we didn't make it this time." But thank God we didn't make it to Thailand or else we would have left my two brothers behind; we couldn't afford to bring them too.

We didn't leave Cambodia until I was about eight years old. We got sponsored to come to the United States. Originally we were going to go to France but, at the last minute, my mother was told that education was much better in the States so we moved here. She is all about education, and not just education for learning math or science, but education in the sense of constantly bettering yourself and learning about your surroundings.

We ended up settling in Connecticut, where I went to junior high and high school. Then I went off to college, which lasted for six years. I transferred, I dropped out, that kind of thing. I knew it was important to get an education but I didn't really know what I wanted to do. At one point, when all my friends had graduated and I still wasn't done, I called my brother and told him I was going to Boston to live with my girlfriend at the time. He said, "Well, I'm starting a new business. It's this sea urchin thing, if you want to help out." I had no idea what the hell I was doing, but I thought I would spend maybe twenty hours a week helping him while I figured out what I wanted to do.

This "sea urchin thing" ended up being my entire existence for two years. The roe of the sea urchin, also called "uni," is an incredibly valuable food product. So my brother's idea was for us to be traders who would buy sea urchin from the divers, get it processed, and sell the uni, usually to the Japanese who want it for sushi. I knew nothing about this, but I figured my brother must have learned a lot about it already. It turns out, he knew about as much as I did. That's the reason why I got so involved and why I kept going; if I didn't, my brother was going to get shit on. I had to learn how to do this.

On a typical day we'd drive from Massachusetts to Maine, which would take about two to four hours. We'd figure out where the sea urchin divers were that day—they were divers, not fishermen—they literally dove down and grabbed all the sea urchins they could. We'd buy the sea urchins from these divers, have a truck come and pick them up, and then we would either sell them to a processing plant in Massachusetts or we would rent out a processing plant and their workers, process the uni, and then try to sell it to Japan ourselves.

In the beginning, I followed my brother around and I watched his mistakes. I didn't talk to any of the divers at first, I just went and tried to learn the look and taste of sea urchins that other people were buying. Then I started to become friends with the sea urchin processors and I told them I would work for them for free for a few days because I just wanted to learn more.

Buying these sea urchins was an incredibly intense process. You had to be at the dock right when the divers came in and you had to understand everything about the sea urchin itself or they would try to cheat you. When you're shopping you can only crack open a few of the sea urchins to look at the roe and see if it is good or not. The divers would top their bags with the best ones and tell you they had a good catch, but then you'd go get it processed and find out that 80 percent of what you bought sucked and you just lost a ton of money. I learned exactly what to look for: The first thing you do is you look for color and size. You want bright orange roe with a hint of red or yellow and then very big eggs that are nice and tight and large. Those are the ones that are sought after. Then you negotiate with the diver, try to get a good rate, and do this all in whispers so no one else can hear you. There were about twenty divers in the area and at one point I knew them all by name and had relationships, good or bad, with each of them.

All of this buying happened in cold, hard cash. We would carry ten to twenty thousand dollars in cash and just buy stuff on the spot. If we spent twenty thousand, it meant we were expecting to get at least sixty thousand when that stuff traded at market. It was such a gamble—you could be loaded with cash one day, and then lose it all the next.

It was exhausting. I would literally go to sleep for two

hours, in my car, and then get up and do another full day. After two seasons, I just couldn't take it anymore and I said to my brother, "Look, I was supposed to come in and just help you. I got very involved because I care about you and obviously I wanted to do the right thing and that was to learn it and do it well." And he said, "I know, I know." I left and he continued on for a few years until he closed the business.

At the end of the day, what the sea urchin business taught me is the same thing that my mom taught me: that learning is important; that you can't succeed without it; and that most of the time you have to figure it out yourself, you have to chase down your own education. Everything I've done since then has been self-taught.

I own restaurants now, and just like everything else in my life, I jumped into that. I had waited tables and knew a bit about wine when I decided I wanted to open a Cambodian restaurant in New York City. But I could not find a cook for the restaurant to save my life. The cooks I found were either very old school or they knew nothing about cooking this kind of food. So I said, "You know what, I guess I'm going to learn how to be a cook." I didn't learn techniques from the best; I didn't go to school and learn how to run a restaurant; I didn't go to school to learn how to cut up a fish a certain way or braise for a certain amount of time. I had to learn all of these things on my own, basically by trial and error. I don't know if that's a good thing or a bad thing, but it's the way I learned everything. To me, it's normal.

——RATHA CHAUPOLY, *forty-three, is the co-owner of Num Pang, a Cambodian sandwich shop that was named "the best sandwich of 2013"* by The Village Voice. *Num Pang has six locations in New York City and an upcoming cookbook.*

WHEN BUSINESS MEETS PLEASURE

The Fond Memories

The Retail Romance

2003

When I was sixteen my older sister and her friends worked at the coolest store in the mall. It was a clothing store that specialized in the sort of preppy-but-skimpy clothes that all the popular kids were wearing. I wanted to work there so badly. Like a lot of teenage girls I was obsessed with clothes and boys and being popular and I knew a job at this store was the key to all of those things. The store had a reputation for only hiring really good-looking people, so getting a job there was a major boost to your social status and a chance to meet hot guys. Plus, you got an amazing discount on the clothes. The catch was that you had to be seventeen to apply. Of course, the day after I turned seventeen I went into the store and applied for a job.

It was a pretty standard application, but then came the interview, where they had me sit in a circle with a group of people and they asked all sorts of offbeat interview questions. They asked us that classic question "If you're stranded on a desert island what is the one thing you would bring?" which is just so dumb. I said "suntan lotion" and I remember leaving the interview and kicking myself about what a lame answer that was. My sister agreed. But I got the job anyway.

Of course, before I could start I needed to do some serious shopping. We didn't have uniforms but we did have a dress code and it involved wearing only clothes they sold at that store. We weren't allowed to wear any black, only light pink and browns and khakis and whites. For shoes you could only wear flip-flops, Ugg boots, or Converse sneakers in navy blue or white. Cargo was a huge trend at the time so for my first day I picked out these super baggy flare-leg cargo pants and a really tight, pink tank top.

It was a very easy job; there wasn't a huge learning curve or a lot of responsibilities. As a sales associate I had to unlock dressing rooms, run the cash register, and just sort of stand in my assigned zone and monitor what was going on. Some days they would have the girls stand in the boys' section and the boys stand in the girls' section. It was pretty awkward for us, but I think the idea was that guys were going to want cute girls around them when they were shopping and then maybe they'd buy more stuff.

On big shopping days, like weekends or Black Friday, they would have "greeters" at the front of the store. This was usually a really buff, shirtless guy and a girl in some sort of skimpy outfit like short shorts and a tank top. The managers always chose the most attractive people for this job, so if you were a greeter for a day you felt pretty good about yourself. On the flip side, the less attractive people were always assigned to do stock in the back.

All the employees at this store were in high school or fresh out of high school and all the managers were in their mid-twenties; there was maybe one thirty-year-old who was the oldest person at the store. Because of the easy workload and the young, laid-back coworkers, working there was tons of fun. I loved it. We'd have these huge staff parties where everyone would get super drunk together and we'd all sleep over at someone's house; sometimes I didn't even know whose house it was. There was a staff softball team that had games followed by, of course, more parties.

I got to know everyone really well but there was one guy, a manager, who I had a huge crush on. He was super tall and buff—you could tell he worked out all the time—and had pretty eyes. I mean, I guess he was pretty basic-looking, but he did have really big muscles.

I'd always look forward to the shifts we had together because we'd flirt like crazy, which basically meant just talking and teasing each other a lot. On days I knew he'd be working I'd always wear my shortest miniskirts. By the time I left that job I think I owned about twenty really short miniskirts.

One of my good girlfriends at work was friends with this manager and so one night the stars aligned and we all went to a concert together. Of course I hung out with him all night and at one point we sort of snuck off into a corner and started to dance together, just the two of us. He ended up driving me home at the end of the night and that's how it all started.

It was a little awkward at work after we hooked up, since no one could know. Not only was he my manager, but I was seventeen and he was twenty-five, so it was technically illegal. But we kept hanging out, just not in public. I would tell my parents I was going to sleep at a friend's house and then go over to his house to spend the night.

He was a sweet and soft-spoken guy, but I think he knew that he was dating a high school girl, so he didn't have to put much effort into it. He wasn't particularly romantic. Though there was this one time he was working at another location and he remembered there was a tube top I really wanted that was all sold out in our store, so he offered to steal one for me. He even called me at work to ask what size I wanted and everything! It was sweet, in a weird way.

The best part of that relationship was how exciting it was for me to be dating this hunky manager, but the worst part was that I couldn't tell anyone. It was the kind of thing I really wanted to brag about but I knew I would get in big trouble if I did. He ended up switching stores three or four months after we started dating and it just sort of fizzled out. Honestly, it was a bit of a relief when he left, because I didn't have to dress up anymore.

——s., *twenty-eight, struggled to find a job after college and briefly considered going back to the clothing store as a manager. She decided not to and now works at a nonprofit for disabled children.*

The Soda Jerk

1954

The first job I had doesn't even exist anymore—a soda jerk.
A soda jerk was someone who would make fountain drinks,
milkshakes, and sundaes at an old-fashioned soda fountain.
It was quintessential 1950s. I never much thought about what
the name "soda jerk" meant, but some people attribute it to
the fact that we would jerk the handle of the soda dispenser
back and forth. If you jerked it forward it would come out at
an ordinary flow and if you jerked it back it would come out
very pressurized. That's just some insider knowledge.

The soda fountain was inside a well-stocked drugstore
called Hollywood Drugs on a corner right near my house. The
drugstore had aspirin and toothpaste and all that stuff, plus
a pharmacy in the back, but the soda fountain was right up
front. The place was run by a guy named Gilbert and so everyone called it Gil's. No one ever called it Hollywood Drugs

unless you were answering the phone, in which case Gil wanted it to sound more businesslike.

All of us kids would congregate on the corner outside of Gil's and it became a big hangout. We'd go in and order fountain drinks and buy little snacks like potato chips. I was there all the time, which is how I got to know Gil, and he offered me a part-time job as a soda jerk just before my thirteenth birthday. It had the huge salary of ninety cents an hour. I was thrilled.

Working at Gil's was a very prestigious position; every kid in the neighborhood would have loved to work there. It was great for me socially. All the girls would come by and there would be an opportunity to exchange loving glances, to the extent someone would do that in the 1950s. A lot of my friends were from families that were more affluent so they didn't need to do anything for extra money, which meant they got to spend a lot of time hanging out with me at the soda fountain.

As a soda jerk I was in charge of operating the soda fountain and making all the different drinks and desserts that were popular back then. We had several different containers with patented syrups that would flavor the sodas. There was something called Green River, which is a thing of the past now. It was a vivid green syrup that made a carbonated lime drink all the kids loved. There was also the chocolate phosphate, a carbonated chocolate drink made with chocolate syrup and soda water. It was our most popular fountain drink and was known as a "chocolate phos."

But the real hallmark of the soda fountain was a classic ice cream soda dessert.

Gil was my mentor. He showed me how to mix the soda with the ice cream so that it came out with a lot of foam. I was very proud of my sodas. They had good foam and a big scoop of ice cream I could get to float right on the top—it looked very appetizing. I always topped every soda I made with whipped cream, and I never asked before I did it because I knew everyone wanted whipped cream. This was before cholesterol.

The year I started working at Gil's, *Playboy* magazine had just been published. It was a new kind of magazine for us in the 1950s and it was highly sought after. Of course it couldn't be kept on the magazine stand because perish the thought that young people would come in and see *Playboy*! Gil was very careful about how he handled these risqué publications: He kept his supply of them behind the counter and they would only be given to adults for purchase. The people in the know would come and ask me, "Do you have the current edition?" and I'd know exactly what they were talking about. *Playboy* was the hot item.

I worked at Gil's all the way through my senior year of high school. Any tips I earned were mine to spend, but the rest of the money was set aside for my college education. Tuition my first year at the University of Illinois was fifty dollars. Imagine that! I always felt good that I had been able to contribute to that and that I could focus on my studies instead of worrying about money during the school year.

My dad, who was a great believer in learning and earning, said that working would create a sense of independence. That it did. My dad was in sales and I knew he was such a qualified guy though I always felt that his strengths were never really fully utilized by the people he worked for. He was an employee all his life. On the other hand, I always thought of Gil as a very entrepreneurial guy who had opened his own drugstore and was doing quite well. My dad never said, "Barry, you should run your own business," but I think he would have loved being his own boss and Gil helped me see that it could be done. Working for him helped me to understand the life of a business owner and ultimately made me believe I could establish something myself instead of working for others.

—BARRY FRIEDMAN, *seventy-three, cofounded his own law firm in Los Angeles. After a fifty-year career as a lawyer, he recently retired.*

The Sausage Prince

2002

The Sausage King wasn't actual royalty, but in my Midwestern town, he was close: He owned the local sausage company that everyone loved. We never ate Ballpark dogs or Oscar Mayer or anything like that—everyone in town ate only the Sausage King's dogs. He was kind of a local celebrity.

The Sausage King was probably in his late sixties when I first met him. His daughter and I had become buddies at school and I was always hanging around their house. It was a palatial Midwestern mansion on one of the fanciest cul-de-sacs in town; we called it the Sausage Palace. He and I hadn't really talked much. He'd maybe said hi to me a few times from his chair where he was watching the news and chomping on an unlit cigar, but I was really just a random teenage boy who was at his house all the time.

As my sophomore year in high school came to a close

I started looking for a summer job, putting in applications at restaurants and that kind of thing. Then one day my friend said, "Go talk to my dad. I told him you needed a job." So I went back into the Sausage King's office, where he was leaning back in a chair behind his desk. He said, "You need work?" and I said, "I'm looking . . ." And he was like, "All right, well, I'll get you something at the sausage company, and you can help out around my house too." Just like that, I had a job.

I started off at the retail store, working as a stock boy and doing things like turning the mustard labels so they all faced the right way on the shelves. I eventually moved up the ranks to work wholesale, stacking pallets in the warehouse and that kind of thing. But my favorite part of the job was the work I did for the Sausage King personally. I would do landscaping or clean up around his yard or wash his yacht; just a lot of random manual labor that he needed me for. Sometimes I'd just hang out with him while he ran errands. And I'd do all of this after putting in a shift at the sausage company. So my first summer job was like a sixty-hour-a-week endeavor.

Working for the Sausage King was my first time really being held accountable for something. He was a businessman, so when he said he wanted something done, he expected that I would find a way to do it. I remember he had these two birch trees in his front yard and they had both died. They were huge, even taller than the house, but he didn't want to tear them out—he wanted to use them for an art project. So he told me his vision; he said, "I want you to saw off all the dead limbs so you just have two huge stalks, and then I want you to paint them purple and hang a bunch of bird feeders from them." And I just looked at him and was like, "This is impossible. How will I get up there? How do you even paint a tree? This cannot be done."

But his attitude toward me was just, "Of course you're going to do it. You're going to figure out a way and it's going to get done." There wasn't really another option. I wasn't just a random friend of his daughter's anymore, I was an employee and I just had to figure out how to get the job done. For the birch tree project, it basically involved me dangling on a ladder too far up, about to collapse and break my neck. But I did it and, in the end, it actually looked fantastic. Kooky, but fantastic.

I worked for the Sausage King throughout high school and over the years he became kind of like a third grandpa to me. His story was really the stuff of legend: His parents were Hungarian immigrants who had started the business back in the 1940s as just kind of a mom-and-pop sausage shop, but he was incredibly ambitious and wanted to make it something bigger. He never went to college or anything; he went to night classes for a couple of years at the local community college to learn business stuff, and then took the reins from his dad and just kind of became a titan. Now his name was on local community centers and he even had a room at a museum named after him.

I, on the other hand, was a pretty middle-class kid. I grew up in a house with four siblings and both of my parents were teachers, so spending time with the Sausage King was really seeing how the other half lived. And it was awesome. He ate well and lived in a big, beautiful house and drove a Bentley. We'd drink fancy wine and brandy after dinner, even on weeknights.

He would also give me a lot of advice about relationships. He was on his third marriage so I think he was really excited to impart all the wisdom he'd learned. He had just read *Men Are from Mars, Women Are from Venus,* so he'd go on these long monologues about how men and women communicate differently and it's all about understanding that. These talks usually came in the car after we'd snuck out of the house because his wife had told him not to get Burger King and we were on our way to Burger King together.

My senior year of high school, I asked his daughter to the prom. That date was awesome because we got to take the forty-two-foot yacht that I had cleaned the day before and sail it on the lake to the prom venue. It was really fancy, and there were appetizers on the boat and everything. Of course, the food was all sausage. On my last day working that summer, before I went off to college, he wrote me a check for two hundred bucks that I used to buy books for school. I called it the Sausage King Scholarship Fund.

—M., *twenty-six, is a magazine editor in New York City. For his birthday last year his mother sent him an eight-pack of franks, mustard, and two packs of sausage from the Sausage King's company.*

The Gun-Club Girl

I have one sister. It's just the two of us, but our dad is very much a man's man. He hunts and fishes and shoots trap, that sort of thing. He is definitely someone who was meant to have a son. When I was younger I was always trying to be the son he never had: I'd go hunting and fishing with him around our small town in Washington, so when I was thirteen years old and my dad told me they needed help at the local gun club, I jumped at the chance.

My job was to set trap for the shooters. This meant I would climb down into the trap house and place a clay disc called a clay bird onto a swaying metal arm. When the scorekeeper gave the signal, the metal arm would fling the clay bird up in the air, and the shooter would aim for it and shoot. Each shooter would get the chance to shoot twenty-five clay birds per round. Every week there was a tabulation that ran in the newspaper and at the end of the season prizes were awarded. People took it pretty seriously, especially my dad, who was often the club's highest-scoring shooter.

Trapshooting season is during the winter, from January to March. Shooting started early in the morning, around 9:00 a.m. So all winter long I woke up at 6:00 a.m. on Saturdays and drove down to the gun club with my dad, with a stop for doughnuts, of course. When it was time for me to go into the trap house and get to work, the shooters would yell, "Get down in your hole, troll!"

I was the first girl they'd ever had working down in the trap house, but everyone still called me the "trap boy." The guys at the gun club were my father's age but I would get to joke around with them, which made me feel pretty cool, like I was one of the guys. That was the best part of the job.

The worst part was screwing up the trap setting. There's a really specific part of the metal arm where you have to put the clay bird. If I got it a little bit off in either direction the arm would fling it against the wall and the bird would shatter all over the trap house, about four feet from my face. This would happen about two or three times a day. I guess technically it was dangerous because I could have gotten hit by some of the shrapnel, but that just never happened. It was more just a scary noise.

Everyone always said I was the best trap boy they ever had, and I think that was because I was really careful and precise—I didn't want to have those birds shatter in front of me. I think that was my advantage, being a girl: We're more detail-oriented. A lot of the boys who had worked there be-

fore me were there because they liked shooting and wanted
to shoot a round on their break. As a result, they didn't care
much about work. But I actually took my role very seriously
and wanted to do a good job. I'd be down in the hole for
about four hours a day in the freezing cold, setting trap again
and again. I got one lunch break for cheeseburgers in the
clubhouse. Getting that burger was just the best thing ever; it
always felt like the most amazing food I had ever tasted. And
then I had to get back in my hole. It was a tough, uncomfortable, and stressful job at times but it felt like such a treat to
make money, when most of our friends were not. I earned
about eight dollars an hour, which is a lot for a thirteen-year-
old who otherwise wouldn't be working at all.

When I started setting traps I had never even shot a rifle.
I didn't get into that until a few years later. Now I live on the
other side of the country and I work at a women's magazine,
but when I go home I still go shooting with my dad. Last
summer my boyfriend came home with me for the first time
and we went out shooting. My boyfriend was born and raised
in Brooklyn so he's very much a city boy and had never shot
a gun before. The first time he shot, he missed all three of the
targets we had set up. Then it was my turn, and I hit everything, spot on. He was like, "Damn!" (I joked that he better
never mess with me.) That's a secret skill I'll always have, and
it's because of the time I spent at the gun club with my dad
when I was growing up.

—KAYLA WEBLEY, *twenty-nine, is a senior editor at*
Marie Claire *magazine in New York City.*

The Rosie the Riveter

1943

It was a Sunday when I found out that we were at war. That morning we heard something on the radio, but not enough, and we were confused. Who would attack us? Who would bomb Pearl Harbor? That was just unheard of. We lived on the coast of Oregon, where my dad was a military officer at Fort Stevens. He didn't come home that night, and that's when we knew it was serious.

The next morning we all went to school because we didn't know what else to do. The principal called us into the assembly room and we all listened to President Roosevelt's speech. That was when it really hit me. I was a junior in high school at the time, and several of the boys a year above me left school and signed up that very week.

We were proud of the boys. We were proud they wanted to serve the country. There was true patriotism at that time and people really believed in our government, no question. But since I was a girl, there wasn't much I could do. We always promised to write letters, and we did, but that was it.

That summer, my older sister Phyllis wanted to join her husband as a welder in the Kaiser shipyards in Richmond, California. She asked me to come down and be the babysitter for her son, my nephew, who wasn't quite two yet. I took a Greyhound bus down there after school was out. At night, the bus drove past the oil refineries in Rodeo, California, and I saw all the lights and thought, "Wow, is this San Francisco?" I had never seen so many lights before, so I assumed that must be the big city I had heard about.

I stayed at my sister's house that summer and I spent a lot of time out in the front yard playing with my nephew. Sailors were always strolling past, and that was how I met my future husband. He was in the Coast Guard and his buddy lived down the street. We got acquainted and we were engaged by the end of the summer. I didn't go back to Oregon in the fall. Instead, I enrolled in the high school in Richmond and, twelve days after I turned seventeen, in the spring of 1943, we got married. He was a couple of years older and it was kind of difficult to be a married woman in high school. I couldn't really participate in a lot of the high school activities, though he did take me to the senior prom.

My parents had four daughters and we were never pointed toward a career at all. Because we were women we were always going to be homemakers—we weren't expected to do anything else. But after I graduated high school, one of my teachers recommended me for a professional art course at UC Berkeley. It was a six-week course in engineering drawing where we learned to read and draw blueprints.

The day that the program was finished some recruiters from the shipyards came to campus and hired us right out of school. I was still seventeen when I got that job offer and I had to lie about my age and say that I was eighteen. It was really a compliment to know that I had been recommended for the course, and an even bigger compliment to know that I had a talent that could be used in the war effort. It was a huge boost to my ego.

I ended up working in the engineering department at Shipyard Number Three in the Kaiser Shipyards. My office was a big room that had desks for all fifteen of us female draftsmen. Then there were six senior draftsmen, all male, who worked in a separate room. They had been deferred during the draft because of their specialized knowledge; they were real draftsmen who did beautiful architectural drawings. We just did small things that kind of took the load off of them. But they never treated us like we were underlings or anything like that. They were grateful that we could help them and they always called us "draftsmen," not "draftswomen," which I really liked. Everyone was very friendly; it was a wonderful group of first coworkers.

Shipyard Number Three built troop transports. They had built one ship but they had made changes in it, and my job was to help make sure we caught up with those changes for the next ships that were built. For example, in one instance they had used the wrong size bolts and they stuck out so they were a safety hazard. I had my clipboard and my hard hat and I would write down where it was and what the problem was. I'd show my supervisor where it was on the pencil drawing and he would change it for the blueprint.

As a draftsman my top pay was about thirty-five dollars a week, which went a long way back then. Between that and my allotment checks from the military, my husband and I put together enough money to make a deposit on a house. Suddenly, I was a homeowner at age eighteen. I never expected that.

After about a year of working, I found out that I was pregnant. When I announced that I was having a baby and was going to leave, the senior draftsmen gave me a surprise baby shower. I had never heard of men attending a baby shower, much less giving one, so I was just stunned. It was just like a normal baby shower, with cake and sweet cards and all of that. It was very touching.

I didn't come back after I had a baby. I was a young mother and, like I said, I was never really trained to think of myself as having a job. My husband and I were married for nine years before we found out it just wasn't a good mix and got divorced. That was when I got my second job, this time at a five-and-dime store as a cashier.

All the "Rosie the Riveter" talk started around the fiftieth anniversary of Pearl Harbor. We never called ourselves Rosies before then. I wasn't even a riveter and most of the other women were welders. Still, it's a real honor to be thought of in that way, as an important part of the war. We never expected to be recognized as having done something special, because everyone was doing something at that time. Everybody had the same goal: to win the war, get it over, and bring the boys back. We were just doing our job.

—MARIAN SOUSA, *eighty-eight, is a volunteer docent at the Rosie the Riveter WWII Home Front National Historical Park in Richmond, California. Recently, she traveled to Washington, DC, with other "Rosies" to meet President Barack Obama and Vice President Joe Biden and be recognized for their wartime efforts.*

The Newbie Barista

2002

Getting a job at my local coffee shop in Orange County was pretty easy. I went in and filled out an application on Friday, had an interview on Saturday, and heard that I got the job on Sunday. The thing was, I had lied about one little thing during my interview: I said I liked coffee.

I definitely did *not* like coffee. I had tried it once when I was hanging out with some girls I wanted to impress. We stopped at Starbucks or something and so I got a coffee, drank two tiny sips, then threw it away and was like, "Yeah, that was great." But when they asked me during the job interview if I liked coffee, I played it off like, "Oh, I *looooove* coffee. I can't live without it." The kind of things I had heard my dad say, basically. The thing is, I really wanted to like coffee. I was fifteen and I thought of myself as the type of person who would be drinking coffee and talking about Woody Allen movies and how I saw Modest Mouse in a bar somewhere. I couldn't help it that I just didn't like coffee!

On my first day of work I came in really early in the morning, just as the shop was opening. The manager gave me a quick tour and then she said, "Okay, cool, I'm going in the back to count the money, do you want some coffee?" And I go, "Oh yeah, I need coffee." And she said, "Okay, just brew a whole pot." And I go "Oh, okay . . ." Now, I had no idea how to brew coffee. But she showed me where the beans were and explained that they were all already preweighed and measured into the coffee filters, so all I had to do was drop it in and pull the lever. So I did just that: I took the premeasured beans in the filter, dropped it into the industrial-sized brewer, and pulled the lever.

All of a sudden, water just came streaming out. I was thinking to myself, "This doesn't seem right." But it wasn't overflowing or anything, so I just let it go. The process finally finished and I poured myself a cup of coffee. It tasted bad, like it always did in my mind. I dumped some into the sink to make it look like I drank more. Then the manager came back in and poured herself some coffee. That was when I noticed that it really didn't look right. It wasn't dark brown like coffee, it was more like dirty-water brown. She looked at me, took a sip, and then spit it back into her cup, all while maintaining eye contact.

"Okay, I think you did something wrong here," she said. So she opened the coffee machine and looked in it and said, "Hmmm, you didn't grind the beans." And I remember just panicking and thinking, "Oh my God, I'm going to get fired.

Not knowing how to make coffee is definitely something you get fired for at a coffee shop." And then she just started laughing. I kind of mumbled, "Oh . . . You have to grind the beans?" I mean, my dad always used preground Folgers stuff, there was none of this grinding business. I'd never even heard of that.

I was so lucky that everyone who worked at that coffee shop was awesome. Most of the employees went to the local junior college so they were five to ten years older than me, but I was immediately taken in as the little brother of the entire staff. Everyone teased me but it was all in good fun; they really took me under their wing. I was the only one who didn't smoke, so when they'd go outside for their forty-minute smoke breaks, I'd be the one covering and taking care of customers. If I was lucky, I'd get to stand outside with them for a few minutes and get some secondhand smoke. That was fine with me. It was like a second family.

When I first started working at the coffee shop I had to get my mom to drop me off and pick me up. It was so embarrassing. Eventually I earned enough money to buy a truck, which was the goal of getting the job in the first place, but I still kept working, partly because I needed to pay for gas and insurance and partly because I liked my coworkers. By the time I was in my junior year of high school I was working thirty to forty hours a week after school and on weekends.

I worked there throughout high school and, eventually, I learned to like coffee. I started with mochas and worked my way up to lattes and cappuccinos and then finally got into brewed coffee with milk and sugar. It wasn't until about six months ago that I started drinking my coffee black. Now that's all I drink. I really love coffee.

—STEVEN DUPRÉ, *twenty-six, is a video editor for commercials, short films, and music videos. He lives in San Francisco's Mission District, a few blocks away from some of the country's best coffee shops.*

The Victory Farmer

1941

The community I lived in was called The Patch. It was one square block in the middle of nowhere. There was a highway on one side of the block and then a row of small, forty-acre farms all lined up against a river on the other side of the block. I went to school in a two-room schoolhouse that had two teachers and four grades.

I was in fourth grade when World War II broke out. Everyone who was eighteen or older, or looked like they were eighteen or older, went and joined the military. All of a sudden the farmers had no help at all. It was just them; even their sons went into the military. It was a bad depression period right then and the worst of it was in rural areas where there was no industry, so the farmers needed help in the fields. At this point they were calling them Victory Farms, because everything was for the war effort. So our teachers let the boys leave school early to go work in the fields. As a nine-year-old I worked every day of the week except Sunday. In the summertime I worked five or six full days a week, at least forty hours a week. The pay was nine cents an hour, so if I worked a forty-hour week back in 1941 I'd just be able to buy a cup of coffee at Starbucks today.

We planted. We weeded. We did everything. They were small farms and they didn't have machines, maybe one tractor at best. To plant a crop of tomatoes we had to dig holes for seedlings and set them in, then put the stakes in and tie them up, then weed them, then check to be sure they didn't get infested by insects, and then, of course, we harvested. And if you wanted to take any produce home with you at the end of the week, you paid for it. You did not get anything for free.

All of this was done by hand, plant to plant, over acres and acres of land. They would be expensive organic tomatoes today. But those tomatoes were wonderful. They just had this amazing flavor, even when you ate them after they'd been sitting in the hot sun. I can still taste them, but I can't buy them. Tomatoes like that don't exist anymore.

I lived with my grandmother at the time. Things were a little tough. My parents were separated when I was seven, so I was already two years away from having a father. Between my grandmother, mother, cousins, and sister there were seven women in the house; I was the only boy.

At the end of a forty-hour workweek I would come home with my $3.60 and give it all to my grandmother. She would give me a quarter back and the rest went toward our rent, which was eighteen dollars a month. I was fine with my quarter: Movies were ten cents so I would go to one movie, get a candy bar for a nickel, and I still had a dime left for the rest of the week. I felt pretty flush.

My coworkers in the fields were my classmates and one straw boss. The straw boss was an older guy who would kind of push us around a little bit. He was probably sixteen or seventeen, while most of the other laborers were between nine and twelve. It was hard work, but it felt like a game. Everyone would start at the beginning of a row and you didn't want to be the last guy. Sometimes you were on your knees all day weeding, but if you saw you were the last one, you knew you had to speed up.

I learned a few things out there in the field. First, I learned how to smoke. One of the fertilizers we used was tobacco stalks that were baled up and shipped in from the South. We'd tear open a bale of tobacco stalks and peel off all the tiny bits of leaves still on there. Then we'd roll it in newspaper and smoke it. We'd smoke this uncured, raw tobacco. I mean, it would knock your head in the creek. We'd get dizzy and groggy and nauseated. Oh my God, the stuff that we were inhaling, without even a filter.

Second, I learned how to hustle because there was no such thing as being a lagger. If the farmer saw somebody wasn't holding up their end, he would scold them. And if they still were too slow, they were fired. That was it. It was just, "This is your last day. Get out." They weren't hesitant to do something like that. So you learned how to respect the boss, and I carried that all through my life. When I was in the military,

I understood what higher rank meant and when it came to working on a production line I understood that the boss is the boss. Right or wrong, he's still the boss.

—BOB MITCHELL, *eighty-one, is a retired dress-pattern maker in New York City.*

The Happiest Worker on Earth

2000

I grew up fifteen minutes from Disneyland. It was every kid's dream. Disneyland was a big part of our childhood, and we often got season passes. My parents were immigrants, so whenever we had guests visiting from India, or really from anywhere, Disneyland was the destination.

My brother, my sister, and I all learned the park inside and out. I can't remember a time when I didn't know every street and ride and restaurant in Disneyland. In fact, I can't even remember ever looking at a map—it was just ingrained in me from such a young age. I couldn't get lost in that park if I tried.

As I got older, my parents never pushed me to get a summer job. In fact, I'd say they discouraged it. They said I had the rest of my life to work, and I should just study and enjoy life now. So I never really thought about it until the end of high school, the summer before I went off to Georgetown for college. I was feeling a little bit antsy, and having never worked before, I wanted to see what it was like. But of course I wanted to have fun too, so Disneyland was the first place that came to mind.

The application process was fairly simple. I filled out a form and went to a thirty-minute interview. I left out the part where I was going to college in the fall; I was worried it would hurt my chances if they knew I was leaving. Anyway, it worked—they ran a few background checks and that was it. I got the job.

I got to rank which positions I was most interested in and I rated being a ride operator first, but in the end I was picked as an "outdoor vendor," also known as "the person who sells you the snacks." I mostly sold frozen lemonade or drinks, but I would also do cotton candy from time to time.

Technically, we weren't called "employees"; we were called "cast members." And no one was a "customer"—they were always a "guest." As soon as you arrived in the park—which was considered anywhere a guest could see you—you were "onstage." Everyone working at Disneyland considered themselves a performer in some sense. We were either "onstage" or "offstage."

If you've ever been to Disneyland, you'll notice that things there are pretty seamless. You never see the background stuff. You don't see employees checking in, changing shifts, or any of those everyday tasks. All of that happens offstage. You'd never see an employee eating at any restaurant near a guest, because we had our own separate restaurants. If you pay attention next time you go you'll see people slipping in and out of doors all over the park. They're marked with little signs that say "cast members only"—those are the doors we'd use to get offstage. It was a well-oiled machine.

I'd check in offstage and get my uniform there—mine was a green-and-red shirt with a big Mickey head on it that I felt really proud to wear. Then I'd walk across the park to pick up my vendor cart. But before I could even touch the vendor cart for the first time, I had to go through a ton of training.

Of all the things I learned at Disneyland, the training is probably what stuck with me the most. It was shocking how unbelievably focused they are on a good customer experience. It is not an act: They really want people to be having the best time *ever*. We were taught that if someone came up to us and had an empty frozen lemonade cup and said they spilled it, you gave them a new one and tried to make them feel better, no questions asked. Rather than trying to get the most dollars out of a situation like that, it was really "How do we maximize the happiness of this person?"

I think the terminology they used helped it become more natural for workers. When you refer to yourself as a "performer" it's very different from thinking of yourself as an "employee" who is there to make a wage. If you are a performer, then actually putting on a good show and making people happy is a goal in itself. They made sure that was how we measured ourselves rather than using the metrics of how many lemonades we sold or anything like that.

I'll always remember the first time I saw a character behind the scenes. It was Mickey. He had just walked off-stage and he took off his head—which, even though I knew there were real people inside, still kind of freaked me out—and it was a girl! I laughed out loud. Turns out, most of the Mickeys are women because they have to be a certain height, and they have to be very expressive and friendly. Still, I understood why they didn't want the guests to see that.

The biggest compliment I can give Disneyland is that, even after working there for a summer, I still hold it in such high esteem and it's still one of my favorite places. After seeing how the magic happens I still appreciate it just as much. I really didn't have to be told to be happy most days, I just was. Nothing could get to me. Sometimes people would complain about the prices, but when you're charging four dollars for a soda you're bound to get some snide remarks. Still, compared to other jobs I have had since, there is something really great about seeing the impact of your work right there, where you can see the smile you are putting on someone's face. You're really being a part of their day.

After I graduated from college I did investment banking and then private equity in New York City, and I always missed that feeling of making people happy. Since I graduated from business school I've been more into start-ups. Working at a smaller place means I have been able to directly see how I'm affecting a customer or user. Weirdly, it's kind of getting back to my Disneyland roots.

>—E., *thirty-two, is the founder of his own company.*
>*Though he no longer lives in Southern California, he still*
>*visits Disneyland when he goes back to see his family.*

The Rebel at the Rectory

2001

I was a frustrated Catholic schoolgirl, which I guess sounds kind of clichéd. The thing is, I really wanted to feel powerful and be independent but I couldn't even drive yet. I decided if I got a job I could at least be making my own money, so I scored a summer position at the only place I knew anything about: my Catholic school. I worked as an administrative assistant in the rectory.

A rectory is a residential dwelling where priests and deacons live. It's usually attached to the church, or at least close to a church, and it has the priests' bedrooms, their kitchen, their bathroom, everything. This one had some offices on the ground floor and that's where I worked. It was a little strange because I would occasionally see the priests there. That was like seeing your teacher outside of school, which is always weird to begin with, except the priests were in their own home, which made it even weirder. They always wore those white clerical collars like they did at Mass on Sundays, even when they were just sitting down and eating lunch or something.

I was super excited to have a job, and it felt even more awesome when I realized I was good at it. My boss, Kris, was the mom of a former student. She worked in the office full time and she definitely gave off that approachable soccer mom vibe. I'd check in with her every morning, and she would give me some projects, and then I would go into my own office—I had my own desk with a computer and everything.

My main tasks were organizing newsletters, stamping mailers, and updating some databases of church members and alumnae. All of these projects were right up my alley. I was naturally very organized and a super-fast typist from spending all this time on Instant Messenger chatting with friends. Kris was very forthcoming with positive affirmation and I totally fed off that. She was always telling me what a great job I was doing and I ate up her praise.

Once, after a particularly well-done task, she said in kind of a stage whisper, "You know, if you ever want a treat, the priest keeps Famous Amos cookies in the kitchen." Of course this was the priests' personal stash of cookies and they weren't really for us, but once I knew they were there, there was no going back. I would sneak in and nose around in the cabinets until I found these cookies and just grab handfuls of them every day. It was bliss.

Anyway, at that point in my life that was about as rebellious as I had ever been: stealing cookies from a priest. But that summer I became really good friends with the queen bee of my middle school, Amy. She was literally everything I wanted to be, and she, of course, did not have a summer job. She just did whatever she wanted.

Amy was dating this guy Craig, who we spent a lot of time with, and one day he was like, "Hey, you gotta meet my friend Matt." It was love at first sight. Matt and I kissed and I was straight-up obsessed from that moment on. I thought he was the greatest thing on earth.

Matt was this elusive guy who didn't go to our school, he didn't even go to a Christian school. In fact, he was maybe Jewish, no one really knew. It was just so, so forbidden. But that became my new summer routine: work at the rectory from nine to two, then have my dad pick me up and drop me off at Craig's house, where we'd all hang out. By "hang out" I mean soak in the hot tub for hours and hours on end and then make out after it got dark. I thought it was so great because I felt like, "Wow, I just left church and a half hour later I'm in the hot tub with a guy who is going to kiss me."

After a few weeks of this, I had Amy e-mail Matt all these questions about what he thought of me. He wrote back, "Why are you asking me this?" without answering any of the questions. It quickly became obvious to everyone, including me, that he loved Amy. So we would all hang out together, and Matt and I continued to make out, but it was pretty clear that he only did that so he could continue to spend time with Amy. I continued to pretend like I didn't notice or care.

Matt and I made out all the time, often in public. Then

one Thursday night it went a little too far and I woke up with a humongous hickey on my neck. I immediately called my older cousin, who was so cool and would totally know what to do. She told me to use concealer to cover it up, and to wear a turtleneck.

So I showed up to work in the middle of summer wearing a turtleneck. I thought I was a clever genius, but Kris was immediately like, "Oh my gosh, what happened to your neck?" I told her I fell down the stairs, which, of course, sounded absolutely insane.

When Kris left for lunch I snuck into the rectory kitchen and filled a plastic bag with ice and stuck it in the turtleneck of my shirt thinking that the ice would help the bruising go away. So I was sitting there with a bag of ice stuffed into my turtleneck and concealer dripping off everywhere and you might think this was a big low point for me but, actually, I felt incredible. I mean, here I am working and being responsible but also doing whatever the fuck I wanted. It was awesome.

That summer, I really enjoyed the experience of being two things at once—a rebellious teenage girl and a really hard worker at church. That job gave me a real sense of independence because it made it clear that parents had no dominion over me there: Kris was my boss and I had earned her trust and that was all that mattered. I certainly felt entitled to my paycheck and I felt very connected to what I hoped a grown-up version of myself would be. It was like playing dress-up. Even now, I still have that rebellious streak that likes to be busy and professional at work but then lets loose with friends on weekends. But there will be no more guys like Matt in my life!

—G., *twenty-seven, is a fashion copywriter. She lives in New York City.*

The Glamorous Gofer

1962

I am a born New Yorker from the old-fashioned Italian-Catholic set that lived at home with our parents. I never had the wonderful frisky days that I gave my children and I was never really allowed to leave Manhattan.

Originally I had wanted to be an actress but my mother just refused that. When I was sixteen my grandfather thought there could be a chance for me to be in his line of work, the fashion business. He owned a men's haberdashery in Rockefeller Plaza. That summer he approached my mother and said, "How would you feel if she came with me to Paris and then stayed to be a pin girl for my friend Coco Chanel?" And my mother said, "No, that is absolutely unheard of." She thought it was inappropriate for a young girl to be working and unchaperoned in Paris. Looking back, I always wonder what would have happened if I had been allowed to go.

Instead, I graduated high school and went straight to art school. I studied fine arts, fashion, and interiors at the Parsons School of Design. In the summer I found a job at Condé Nast that paid three cents a day and a bowl of rice. The job title was "summer rover"—very glamorous—and the task was to be the private secretary of the publisher of *House & Garden*. My parents approved because Condé Nast was, and probably still is, a launching pad. It's technically a media company but, for young people, it's sort of an Ivy League pedigree for fashion, design, and the arts. If you got there, then you were able to open a lot of other doors for yourself.

I did my job very well that summer because it was terribly boring. I had to answer his phone and give him his pills every four hours and just sort of mind the desk outside of his office. I was bored all day, so what did I do? I read magazines! And that's how I discovered fashion magazines. I did that for just the summer, which was truly all I could bear, and then I said good-bye.

When I finished with Parsons I went back to Condé Nast and they said to me, "Great, we have another terrific spot for you because you were so good at managing the front desk." And I was thinking, "Well, I didn't really do anything . . ." But for four cents a day and a bowl of rice, I got a job that was just a little bit better than a gofer. My job was to sit outside the office of a new gentleman who was coming in to Condé Nast. His identity was not revealed to me during job discussions, but I had strict directions on what to do: Nobody was allowed to see him without his permission. When he said something it had to be done instantly. His phone had to be answered in one ring. I thought, "God forbid I have to go to the ladies' room, I'll be finished!"

I found out the night before that the man was the son of the Newhouses, who owned the entire corporation. It was S. I. Newhouse, who is now the chairman of Condé Nast. Back then he was just coming in from the *Newark Daily Ledger,* which was a newspaper his family also owned, and he was going to take over the magazines. This was the beginning of S.I.'s enormous rise to power.

When he walked in that first day I felt I should stand up as soon as I saw him. As it turned out, he was about my height, which is five foot three. Plus, with all due respect to S.I., he would never win a prize for being handsome—people often say he looks like a monkey. But he had enormous energy and so much kindness. I think he got a kick out of the fact that I was told, "You have to *run* when he calls you and *run* when the phone rings," which I took very literally. Answering the phone turned out to be one of my favorite parts of the job because it was all the swells of New York calling. Barbara Walters called nearly every day—it was just thrilling. His whole social retinue was people I had read about in the newspaper.

My desk was right in between the offices for *Vogue* and *Glamour.* All of the offices were very simple: They had highly shined floors with long corridors of little cubbyhole offices. Even the editor in chief didn't have an office to die for, and the beauty editor was crammed into a small office with her assistant. Everyone had busy desks and there were lots of young girls like me who wanted to go into fashion.

Of course, in Condé Nast in those days you had to have a certain look. You had to dress a certain way. If you dressed abominably, you were told that you were dressed abominably, but if you dressed well, people let you know that you made the grade. Everything was examined, from the way you folded your scarf to which shoes you wore with which purse. If it wasn't on point, the editors would look you up and down and just sigh. You knew you didn't wear that again. Or they'd just come right out and tell you. I had one editor say to me, "Listen to me, you *never* put on those shoes with that bag. It's just not done. So don't ever come like that again. Oh, and you have too much makeup on."

I caught on quickly, in part because my grandfather gave me some wonderful advice. He always told me that you can learn a lot about who someone is by looking at their shoes. One evening I got on the elevator to go home and this little chubby old lady got on with me and I looked down and she had the most remarkable green alligator shoes. I can remember them to this day. I have never seen shoes like that in my life. And I smiled at her because I thought, "This woman has got to be so important, her shoes are so incredible." She turned out to be the editor in chief of *Vogue*, Jessica Daves.

I saw *The Devil Wears Prada* and I just thought that was so spot on. People were terrified of the editors. That's why it was great that I was working for S. I. Newhouse, because he was a sweetheart and he was not taken in with all this. I loved my time there, but eventually I had to move on and become more independent in my career. I always say that a first job is like a first love: It's very rare that you hit it right the first time.

—JOJO CAPECE *is an artist, sculptor, and author. She has lived in Rome, England, and Turkey and now resides in San Francisco.*

The Hippie in Training

1966

I had been going to this summer camp in rural Pennsylvania for as long as I could remember. When I turned fourteen, I was officially too old to be a camper, but not old enough to be a counselor. I wouldn't dream of skipping a summer, so I got a job being a dishwasher, along with six other former campers.

Our job was to wash the dishes and pots and pans after every meal. It was incredibly hot and humid that summer and we used one of those restaurant dishwashers where you load a rack and slide it into this steaming dishwasher, then pull it out with your bare hands when the dishes are still burning hot. I was just a pool of sweat that whole summer. But because I was a dishwasher, I had a lot more freedom than when I was a camper. Probably too much freedom. During the day all we had to do was show up to our shifts after meals. We didn't have any other jobs and we weren't even expected to participate in camp life. I'm not even sure that anyone really had their eyes on us, we sort of slipped through the cracks— not much supervision and not much responsibility.

This was the summer of 1966, when the world was just beginning to change. JFK had been shot, the Beatles were getting big, and the first major demonstrations against the Vietnam War had just happened. American society was just starting to shift into what we now think of as "the hippie era." That summer I went from being pretty buttoned up and buttoned down to having flowing hair and questioning authority. I took off my bra after an older counselor told me that it was a binding, constricting garment put on us by the patriarchy, and I don't think I put it back on again until I was about twenty-eight.

I was really busy trying to come off as more sophisticated than I felt that summer. I couldn't be bothered with any of the little kids at the summer camp; I was very focused on the counselors who were a few years older than me, and wanted to be accepted by them. I mean, fourteen is really a terrible age. I'm surprised that any of us survive it.

Of course, this was also the summer that I smoked my first joint. It was early in the season and I was hanging out in the staff lounge where the counselors were and somebody was passing a joint around. I wanted to be seen as cool so I took a hit. Nothing happened. Nothing happened for the first four or five times. And then something *did* happen and it was like, "Oh, I get it now. This is what they're all talking about." I smoked pot a lot that summer, though I never really liked being high. It always made me more paranoid and shier than I was, and I was already pretty self-conscious.

It was also the summer that I had my first kiss. What I remember most about that experience was how it made me not want to have a second one. But this kid John and I had a lot in common: We had gone to camp together forever; we were both dishwashers that summer; and, best of all, we both had new braces that year. One night we had gone to get what was probably a post-joint snack of peanut butter and jelly in the kitchen where we worked. So we were eating these sandwiches when, out of the blue, he kissed me with his peanut butter mouth. It was pretty awful. He didn't know how to kiss, I didn't know how to kiss . . . It was kind of gross. It was one kiss, and then a little bit of tongue experimentation, which was *really* gross. I think we both kind of recoiled a little bit after it happened, like, "This is not what I expected this was going to be like." We never kissed each other again. We were still friends afterward, but there was no spark. If there had been a spark, I think the peanut butter breath and braces would have killed it.

When I came home after that summer I felt like I had a secret, maybe a whole secret life that involved smoking and kissing. But soon it was back to normal, and I didn't feel like I had gained any real ground in terms of getting cooler and more sophisticated. It seemed like everyone was still ahead of me and I was just as self-conscious and shy as I always had been. But the world had cracked open a little bit that summer, and I knew a bit more about how things worked when there were no grown-ups around.

If I could change one thing about that time period, I would put my damn bra on. The sixties and seventies were a long time to go without a bra when you have big breasts! I'd be interested to see what the difference in my life would be if I had had more support.

—K., *sixty-three, became a junior counselor the following summer and then a full-fledged counselor. She's now a writer in Boston.*

Acknowledgments

A thank-you, first of all, to everyone who shared his or her first-job stories with me. It's stating the obvious to say that, without you, this book would not be possible. You took the time to tell me the funny, traumatic, and embarrassing memories (including the ones you would probably rather forget) that are the heart of this book, and I am so grateful. May your collected wisdom and hard-earned lessons inspire many others at their first jobs!

Thanks to all of the story scouts who sent great tales my way: Tamar Levine, Alissa Dos Santos, Michelle Morrison, Jaime Harper, Camilla Ferenczi, Stephanie Wu, Marissa Conrad, Lauren Honig, Alex Samuel, Alli Lehr, and Andrea Bartz. You made my day.

Thank you, Stephen and P.J. at Picador, for your fantastic insights and endless patience, and thanks, Hanya, my mentor by association, for giving me this opportunity to accrue personhood points.

A thank-you to Erin Hobday and Carla Lalli Music, two of my best-ever bosses, who showed me exactly how wonderful work could be.

Thanks to Eimear for blazing the trail and for helping me realize that every job can be a first job with a good new life plan.

Thank you, Brian, for brewing coffee before early-morning interviews, doing dishes during late-night interviews, and making pit stops for interviews during our vacation. You are an incredible pre-husband.

Thank you, Mom, Dad, Cait, Dan, and Steve, for so, so much. You've been on board with this since I self-published my first book, *The Ghost Who Went Shopping*, at age seven, and I couldn't love you all more.